The Life of
An Ordinary Man
In the Hands of
An Extraordinary God

John Gowan

ISBN 978-1-63903-343-0 (paperback)
ISBN 978-1-68517-254-1 (hardcover)
ISBN 978-1-63903-342-3 (digital)

Christian Faith Publishing, Inc.
832 Park Avenue
Meadville, PA 16335
www.christianfaithpublishing.com

Printed in the United States of America

For our four precious grandchildren—Madison, Samantha, Dane, and Jude.

Contents

Preface

The idea for this book originated years ago when my wife and I tried to get our mothers to fill out a journal we gave to each of them to chronicle their lives. We wanted to know more about what made them who they were—their joys, their struggles, and how they dealt with them. Unfortunately, both of them felt that their stories weren't significant enough to take the time to fill in this journal. We, however, felt that this deprived us of some wonderful insight into their years growing up and seeing how God had been working in their lives. My father-in-law and mother-in-law's stories could really have been made into a movie! While my life story doesn't seem to me to be as interesting or engaging as our parents'—growing up in the Great Depression years and living through the turmoil of World War II, nonetheless—I hope that my life lessons might provide some benefit to my sons and grandchildren and bring glory to God for the way He has worked in my life. I also want to thank my wonderful wife, Elise, for the numerous hours and days that she spent taking dictation for the writing of this book, editing my grammar, and putting it into a Word document. This book couldn't have been written without her.

> Now all praise to God for his wonderful kindness to us and his favor that he has poured out upon us, because we belong to his dearly loved Son. So overflowing is his kindness toward us that he took away all our sins through the blood of his Son, by whom we are saved, and he has showered down upon us the richness of his grace. For how well he understands us and knows what is best for us at all times. (Ephesians 1:6–8 NLT).

CHAPTER 1

Coming to ChristMy Testimony

Hi! My legal name is John William Gowan Sr. Those who don't know me very well call me John. But I really have many names. My friends call me Jack, my sons call me Dad, my grandchildren call me Papa, the youth at church would call me Mr. Jack, and my wife sometimes calls me Punkin. I am an ordinary man and have done nothing extraordinary in my life, but I have been helped along the way by an extraordinary God. He goes by many names as well. I know Him as my Heavenly Father and His Son, Jesus Christ, as my Lord and Savior. But God really has many more names. He was known to the Israelites as Yahweh. He is also known as Emmanuel, which means "God with us." Another name for God is Abba, which is a more familiar name like Daddy, and Jehovah-Jireh, which means "The Lord will provide." These are just a few of the names that represent the many aspects of God's character and nature.

I want to tell you how this extraordinary God has worked in my life throughout the years to guide me, provide for me, comfort me, give me wisdom, and help me through the good times and the bad times. In this book, I will attempt to give you a small sampling of how He has accomplished that in each of the abovementioned areas in my life and how I have drawn closer to Him in the process.

I want it to be clear that this book is not intended to be an autobiography but, as the title states, it is about an awesome God who loves us and is working on our behalf in all circumstances. While I will be attempting to highlight certain events in my life, my purpose is exclusively to show what an awesome God we serve in the hopes that my sons, my grandchildren, and any others who read this book will benefit from my faith journey.

Be very careful never to forget what you have seen God doing for you. May His miracles have a deep and permanent effect upon your lives! Tell your children and your grandchildren about the glorious miracles He did. (Deuteronomy 4:9).

God helped me both prior to my coming to Christ as well as after I committed my life to serving Him. This book is intended therefore to be a testimony to how God has worked in my life, is still working in my life, and I trust will continue to work in my life, as well as in the lives of my sons and their families.

I feel that so many times we fail to comprehend how a loving God is working in and through our lives. We take so much for granted and often fail to see past the present circumstances to the bigger picture. I believe there are miracles happening all around us that we either fail to see or simply take for granted. My intent in writing this book is to encourage my grandchildren to trust God in the big and small things, through the good and bad times, when they can see His answers to their prayers and when they cannot. It is also my desire to show, through the Holy Spirit's help, how important it is for all Christians to share their faith with others—for us to be bold enough to discuss with our friends and colleagues the gospel message.

When I began this writing, we were waiting on the test results of our younger son's MRI, praying with faith and believing God's promise that He does hear and answer our prayers. I have always felt, even before I was a believer, that God was working in my life. And while I have concerns, as any father would, about the outcome of our son's tests, I have faith that my prayers for his healing will be answered. I base this on the thousands of ways that God has answered my prayers in the past.

As far back as I can remember, I recall my mother praying with me nightly the simple prayer of "Now I Lay Me Down to Sleep" and asking God for many requests and seeing my childlike prayers so often answered. When I was eleven years old, I was getting repeated sore throats and ear infections. My mother took me to our family physician who, after examining my throat, said that I needed to have my tonsils removed. He explained to us that my tonsils were extremely large and absolutely needed to come out. At that time, many children were having their tonsils removed, but I was terrified at the thought of having surgery. I prayed to God numerous times that I would not have to have my tonsils removed. I pleaded with my mother to take me to another physician for a second opinion. She was reluctant at the beginning because of the cost, but she finally relented and took me to another doctor. Upon this doctor's examination of my throat, he told both of us, "What tonsils! Your son's tonsils are perfectly normal in size and absolutely do not require surgery." I knew that God had answered my childlike prayer!

In those days, unlike today where they put tubes in children's ears, they lanced both of my eardrums, relieving the pressure. Because I now had tiny holes in my ears, when I would go swimming, water would get in behind my eardrums, causing me to have numerous ear infections. Thus, I seldom went in the water and never learned how to swim. Shortly after the answer to my prayers regarding my tonsils, I had another scary incident, which I took to the Lord in prayer. My mother and dad were building a new home, and in an effort to save money, my father decided to build the kitchen cabinets. He was delivering the cabinets in a stake-bed truck along with a stack of four-by-eight sheets of plywood to be used in the new home. I begged my father to let me ride in the back of the open truck since we were only going a short distance. He instructed me to stay way up front in the bed of the truck, which I did until the final turn onto our street when I walked back between the cabinets and the sheets of plywood. As he rounded the corner, the load shifted, pinning me between the cabinets and the plywood, then breaking my collarbone. Had I been turned the other way, the tremendous weight of the plywood could have more seriously injured me or even killed me. I believe that God once again intervened in my life and spared me. I felt tremendous pain in my right shoulder and could not lift my arm. While I was pretty sure that I had broken my collarbone, I prayed that I would not need surgery. X-rays taken at the hospital showed that my collarbone had been broken in two places and surgery was required. While it appeared that God had not answered my prayer, God, being omniscient, could see far into the future, which I obviously could not. After surgery when they were rolling me off the operating table, the pins in my shoulder broke. A follow-up x-ray showed that I was going to need surgery again! The second surgery required wiring the bones in place since the pins did not hold. I now had to spend five or six days in the hospital instead of just two as originally thought. I was months in recovery with my arm in a sling, which obviously ruined my summer vacation that year. This was another reason why I never learned to swim, and now I had this huge scar on my shoulder, which was a total embarrassment for me. The doctors also told me at this time that I would probably never be able to play football.

While in the hospital, in the adjacent room to mine, I met a girl who was there for the duration of my stay. As her family came in to visit her frequently, I got to meet her older brother, Roger, who was five or six years older than me. He had just received his Eagle Scout badge. The following summer I joined the Boy Scouts and was working on one of my badges, which required me to swim the length of a pool. At Boy Scout camp that summer, as was their customary way at the time of teaching kids how to swim, I was thrown into the deep end of the pool! They reached out to you with a long pole if you weren't able to swim to the other side. After several failed attempts at swimming, I became more and more terrified of the water. At this point, I had given up on ever learning how to swim! The next day, after repeating the same terrifying procedure several more times, I was determined never to enter a pool again when Roger appeared and, seeing my consternation, quickly took me aside and worked with me privately in the shallow end of the pool for the entire afternoon. His encouraging words and patient teaching methods helped me to overcome my fear of the water, and he was actually able to teach me how to swim.

Looking back I now can see that even though God didn't answer my prayer that I would not need surgery on my shoulder, He had a plan to bring me together, through that hospital stay, with the young man who would be able to teach me how to swim. Roger, being much older, was someone I admired; and he was therefore able to help me overcome my fear of the water. Roger also helped me again, much later in life, which I will later share. To me, all of this just exemplifies how God works in each of our lives, as He promised in Romans 8:28 that all things would work together for our good while not necessarily being good.

Early in life, I believed there was a God, but I didn't really know Him; and the only thing I knew about Jesus is that we celebrate His birthday at Christmas. I had no real understanding of who Jesus is because as a family we never discussed anything religious in nature. We attended church sporadically at best, mostly at Christmas, so I had no religious training growing up. I had no knowledge of the significance of Easter or Palm Sunday or anything other than Christmas. While I frequently prayed at night as a child, up to about the age of eleven, it was merely a rote prayer that I recited. After age eleven, my prayers were less frequent and I usually only prayed when I had a problem or thought I had a problem. Prayer was mostly a last resort after I had exhausted all my other options. I didn't understand and certainly hadn't been taught about having a personal relationship with God and that I could talk to Him like I would talk to another person.

My faith journey really began around the age of eleven when my family moved from Cleveland,

Ohio, to New Philadelphia, a small town in north-eastern Ohio, where my dad had taken a job as an industrial engineer after a ten-year career as an aeronautical engineer with the NACA, the forerunner of our current NASA. It was not long after moving there that I met a schoolmate named Al, who became one of my best friends. His father was a physician, and I spent many hours and many nights at his house because we shared so many common interests. I admired Al because he was an excellent student and a decent athlete, much better than I was in both of those areas. As time went on, our being on the football team together helped to cement our friendship as we frequently walked home from practice together, often stopping for a milkshake on the way, discussing girls and all the other things boys talk about. Our shared passion for football definitely brought us closer together. I frequently had dinner at their house and, looking back, one of the things that made a big impression on me was that his family always prayed before meals, not a rote prayer but rather a heartfelt expression of their gratitude for the food and the blessings God had given them. This was something I never experienced in my own home.

As our friendship grew, I came to admire Al more and more for many reasons, but I could never quite discern what made him different until later on in life. As I have retraced my faith walk, I came to realize that Al was the one who planted that first seed of faith. He regularly attended church growing up, while I did not. He seemed to always take the moral high ground, and he had a sense of direction for his life that I lacked.

Even though attending Ohio State University together for a couple of years, we seldom saw each other and drifted apart in those college years. He ended up becoming a doctor and moved out west to begin his practice. As we would get together years later for class reunions, I came to realize that he had a deep personal relationship with Jesus Christ, which he was very open about sharing with me and other classmates. After one of those reunions, he sent me a copy of Max Lucado's book *In the Grip of Grace*. At this point in my life, I was just beginning to grow in my faith.

From the time I moved to New Philadelphia, a small town that revolved around football, I developed a passion for the sport. My heroes in those years were the New Philadelphia High School and Ohio State University football players. I ate, slept, and dreamt football! After graduating from high school, I tried out for Ohio State's football team where I met another young man named Al, who was the second person to impact my life for Christ. Al's older brother had previously attended OSU and was an all-American there and later became an all-pro guard. Al had played football for our main high school rival, but I didn't know him in high school. As we got to know one another better, what initially impressed me about him was the way he handled adversity—better than other players on the team—and challenges and setbacks, like living in the shadow of his famous older brother. Unfortunately, I flunked out of OSU after my freshman year and ended up taking a temporary job with the Ohio Highway Department in my hometown.

Through a set of circumstances that could only have been God-ordained, I ended up on the graveyard shift as a radio dispatcher, working from 11:00 p.m. to 7:00 a.m. Ironically, Al's father was a custodian there and our shifts overlapped. As we were the only two souls there during those hours, I had the opportunity to get to know this faith-filled Christian man on a personal level. He almost always had the radio tuned in to some Christian evangelist. As the majority of nights I had little or no dispatch work, and since I was not a reader, I frequently listened to these Christian messages. This was really my first exposure to the gospel. What I admired most about Al's dad was that he was an

African American with six children, and he and his
wife had managed to see all of them through college, him working as a custodian and his wife as a
housekeeper. He was greatly admired by people in
the community as well. While our shifts only overlapped a couple of hours, this left six hours for me
to ponder in the wee hours of the morning what I
had heard. As Al would stop to visit his dad occa-
sionally, I came to realize that the differences I saw
in him were the result of his Christian upbring-
ing. When I went back to OSU in the spring of
the following year, I could not go out for football
because of health reasons and I never ran into Al
on campus. And no longer being employed by the
Highway Department, I never saw Al's dad again,
but they both had made a lasting impression on
my life. They had watered the seed that had been
planted by my high school friend Al.

The third person who truly cultivated that
seed of faith, many years later, was a boating friend
named Dave. Dave grew up in my hometown and
by now was married with five children and working
as a chiropractor. Dave's dad also was a chidprac-
tor and had been the team physician for our high
school football team. He had treated me when I was
injured my senior year. He was also highly regarded
in the community. By the time I met Dave, I was

also married with two children. Dave and I got to know each other through our common love of sailing, as we were docked right beside one another at our local marina. Our families spent a great deal of time together at a local inland lake, both on the dock and around the evening campfires. Once a summer, we would trailer our boats up to Lake Erie, where we would take a week-long sailboat vacation together, which drew us even closer as friends. By this time, my wife had become a born-again believer and had her women's Bible study praying for my salvation. In fact, they had been praying for a number of years.

Early one morning, while on vacation with Dave and his family and while my wife and boys were still sleeping, I walked up to the marina restaurant to eat breakfast. Walking into the restaurant I noticed Dave sitting there, praying before eating his breakfast. I had long admired Dave for the way he managed the stresses of his practice and his large family. And I always felt that there was something different about him. While I tended to be a worrier, Dave always seemed to have a calmness and an optimistic spirit about him. I later learned that he had a deep faith walk and a trust in God that the Lord would always see him through life's trials. Not long afterward, I started attending a men's Bible study and invited Dave to come, as he had now moved to our neighborhood. I can't put an exact date on when I accepted Christ as my Lord and Savior, but looking back I can see how each of these three men impacted my life for Christ—one planting the seed of faith, the second one watering it, and the third one bringing it to harvest through that simple act of praying before a meal. The light bulb finally went on for me that each of these men I had so admired was a deep man of faith. As I grew in my faith as a baby Christian through this men's study and many conversations with Dave, one of the things Dave taught me, which I have since shared with many others, is his saying, "Keep your eyes on Jesus, and not your fellow man, as your fellow man will let you down every single time." While this seems like such a simple statement, it is certainly not easy to put into practice.

Jesus is the only one we are to look to for strength, guidance, and wisdom; not any pastor, our spouse, or our friends. God's goal for each one of us is to become more Christlike and to grow into a deeper relationship with Him through daily Bible study and prayer, meditating on His Word, and putting His Word into practice. Our human tendency is to try to fix things in our own strength or on the advice of others when Christ wants us to turn every problem, every situation and, in fact, our entire lives over to Him, seeking Him through His Word and the leading of the Holy Spirit.

CHAPTER 2

Spiritual GrowthThe Next Step

While we can never attain a sinless life, we should be growing daily in our Christian walk. Too often, in my estimation, we lead someone to Christ but then fail to continue to disciple them. This often leaves them vulnerable to falling away, because we each need the fellowship of other believers and the spiritual food of God's Word. God wants us to not only come to faith in Christ but also to grow more Christlike. As the parable of the four soils in Matthew 13:19–21 says, "The seed that fell on the hard path represent those who hear the Good News about the kingdom and don't understand it. Then the evil one comes and snatches the seed away from their hearts. The rocky soil represents those who hear the message and receive it with joy. But like young plants in such soil, their roots don't go down very deep. At first they get along fine, but they wilt as soon as they have problems or are persecuted because they believe the word."

My old boss, and later business partner, once said, "All things are either spiraling up or spiraling down." This pertains to everything: countries, cities, businesses, marriages, and our personal growth, both physically and spiritually. There is no such thing as stagnation. Stagnation actually means it is spiraling down. As individuals, physically we are either growing stronger or we are getting weaker. The same applies to our spiritual life as well. We are either drawing closer to God or moving farther away. We are either dying to self and becoming more like Christ or becoming more self-centered and ruled by our flesh.

First Corinthians 9:24–25 says, "Remember that in a race everyone runs, but only one person gets the prize. You also must run in such a way that you will win. All athletes practice strict self-control. They do it to win a prize that will fade away, but we do it for an eternal prize."

We would like our spiritual growth to be a straight line upward, when in fact it is more like a roller coaster with its ups and downs But, unlike a roller coaster, we should always be moving in an upward direction overall. As Dr. Charles Stanley has said in his *In Touch Daily Devotional*[1] regarding the beliefs and practices of genuine believers, "God's commands are not burdensome to those who belong to Christ. Although they fail at times, the overall direction of their life is one of obedience."

About the time I came to Christ, I was blessed to have a pastor who started a men's Bible study and reached out to me to join it. We met weekly for breakfast before work, and we studied the Scriptures together. I was a part of this group for about five years, during which time I did grow spiritually. (My wife says it was painfully slow!) We discussed our common struggles regarding work, family, and our walk with the Lord. I was fortunate to be a part of two other men's groups in the years that followed. The second one I led in our home in Ohio, with the assistance of our new pastor. The third group was here in Florida where I was asked to mentor a group of younger men. Each of these groups either taught or reinforced principles that I have tried to implement in my own life and have sought to share in this book. Men's groups are important not only to learn more about God's Word but also to hold one another accountable. It is in a group like this where you can hopefully find an accountability partner.

---

[1] Charles Stanley, *In Touch: Daily Readings for Devoted Living* (October 26, 2020), 41.

While it is rare to have a true friend that you can feel close enough to express your feelings and struggles, it is something to strive for throughout your life. An attorney friend once told me that you are extremely blessed if you have five really close friends in your lifetime. And it goes without saying that men need male accountability and/or a prayer partner and women need a female. I have found that men have a far more difficult time opening up to one another. It generally takes more time to develop that kind of a relationship, and it usually requires some common interests besides being a Christian. Men don't readily share their innermost thoughts and feelings due to a variety of factors, like pride, insecurity, fear of gossip, or an inability to express themselves well. It has been said that there are five different levels of conversation: level one being things like "How's the weather?" and "What's your favorite restaurant?" and level five being able to discuss the question "How is it with your soul?" In order to get to that *level five relationship*, two men need to share the same core values—those basic Christian values being (1) a personal relationship with Jesus Christ, (2) a belief in the authority of Scripture, (3) a desire to grow in your relationship with Christ, (4) unselfish love, (5) deep loyalty and trustworthiness, and (6) a willingness to be transparent or real with each other.

To grow in our walk with Christ, you have to develop a daily habit of spending time in God's Word. This can be through either a daily devotional or daily Bible reading. I highly recommend a *Life Application Bible*, where the footnotes help to relate your Scripture reading to your daily life. I have also found Charles Stanley's monthly *In Touch Devotional* to be very beneficial to my spiritual growth. I started using his daily devotional shortly after I became a believer and have continued to use it ever since. It has been amazing to me how a particular day's reading so often is relevant to what is going on at that time in my life. I know that is the Holy Spirit speaking to me. And I have found that my whole day goes much better when I start it off with reading my Bible.

Like a daily devotional, the Bible needs to be read daily. I, unfortunately, didn't develop the habit of actual Bible reading, outside of my daily devotional, until about fifteen years after I came to Christ. My first Bible was the King James Version, which I found to be very difficult to understand. The King James Version is probably the most accurate translation from the original manuscripts and is great for memorizing scripture, but it was difficult for a new believer like me to understand. When my wife and sons gave me a New Living Translation, I was amazed at how much easier it was for me to comprehend, and I got a lot more out of it. I didn't read through the entire Bible until even later than that, which I regret! And I am now finding, as I am reading through the New Testament a second time, that I am gaining new insights each time I read it. The Bible is an amazing book, unlike any other, in that it is the divinely inspired Word of God and continues to speak to us throughout our entire life. There is an acronym for the word *Bible* that goes BIBLE—basic instructions before leaving earth.

In Stu Weber's book *Tender Warrior*,[2] he tells the saying of his friend Moishe Rosen who said, "You get a microwave (or a stereo) and you get a book. You get a toaster, you get a book. You get a car, you get a book. You get a life, you get a book." And I would add to that, you get a boat, you get a book. Weber went on to say that we are to think of the Bible as the owner's manual for our life, issued by God, the patent holder.

But God's Word is so much more than just an instruction manual for your life. It is more than just a bunch of rules or dos and don'ts. It is really God's love letter to His children. And to become one of God's children, we have to confess Jesus Christ as

---

[2] Stu Weber, *Tender Warrior* (Multnomah Press, 1993), 37.

our Lord and Savior and receive His Holy Spirit, who will lead us in understanding His Word and incorporating it into our lives. Unlike prayer, where we are expressing our feelings and needs to God, the Bible is God speaking to us, telling His love for us and instructing us on how we are to live our life. The Bible is unlike any other book in that it has more than forty different human authors and was written over a period of about 1500 years. Its authors were divinely inspired, and there is complete harmony within this sacred book. It was the very first book printed on the Gutenberg printing press and has been reprinted more than any other book.

Another way that I felt I grew spiritually was by listening to Christian radio. In my sales job, as I traveled in the car, I would frequently listen to Christian radio stations. There are so many great daily programs on the radio from outstanding pastors like David Jeremiah, Andy Stanley, and Greg Laurie and my favorite ministry, *Focus on the Family*. They often inspired me and helped me to grow spiritually. One of the *Focus on the Family* programs led me to a book by a former football coach from Baylor University named Grant Teaff, *Winning—It's How You Play the Game*.[3] In his book, Coach Teaff quotes a poem by

---

[3]   Grant Teaff, *Winning—It's How You Play the Game* (Word Inc., 1993), 38–39.

John Greenleaf Whittier that I used talking to the
young people at our church.

Don't Quit

When things go wrong as they sometimes will,
And the road you trudge seems all uphill, And
the funds are low and the debts are high
And you want to smile, but you have to sigh. When
care is pressing you down a bit, rest if you must.
But don't you quit.

Life is queer with its twists and turns,
As everyone of us sometimes learns.
Many a failure turns about,
When he might have won had he stuck it out.
Don't give up though the pace seems slow,
you may succeed with another blow.

Success is failure turned inside out,
The silver lining in the cloud of doubt.
You can never tell how close you are.
It may be near when it seems so far.

So stick to the fight when you're hardest
hit. It's when things seem worse
That you must not quit.

I found this poem to be very inspiring, but once I became a believer, I learned that we don't have to go through it alone. Jesus assures us throughout the Bible that "He will never leave us nor forsake us." I have found over the years that knowing that He is always there by our side brings us peace and comfort, even in the most trying of times. Our God is omnipotent, which means He is all-powerful; omniscient, which means He is all-knowing; and omnipresent, which means He is in all places at once. Knowing these incredible qualities of God and that He loved me enough to send His Son to die for me, I realized that He always wants the very best for me. Throughout life we are faced with many choices, two different paths to choose from. Sometimes I chose to go my own way instead of God's way, which really is the essence of sin. Doing what *I* want to do the way *I* want when *I* want. *I* is the center letter in the word *sin*. God's way is most often the more difficult choice but, in the long run, the very best for our life, because He loves us and wants the very best for us.

One of the best examples I can give of this is when I started my company in August 1978. The company was a brokerage for new and used machine tools. Like any start-up company, I needed a new product to sell, and I knew the best way to obtain machine tool lines was to go to the largest machine tool show, which took place in Chicago only once every two years. This show was occurring in September of that year. This left me only several weeks to get a phone number and have business cards printed. The phone company gave me a phone number, which ended in the number 666. Not recognizing the significance of that number at the time, as I was not a believer yet and so had never read the Bible, I went ahead and had business cards printed with that phone number ending in 666. I went to the show and handed out my cards so I was pretty much locked in now to using that number. As I had established some open lines, after the show I continued to hand out cards to many potential customers. In addition, I had stationery printed for business letters and machinery quotations, which also included that phone number.

My wife, already being a born-again believer, informed me that she was not happy with the phone number I had been given. But I was afraid of losing a lot of business, as back in those days that was the only way that customers could reach me. Furthermore, the business was started on a shoestring, so I didn't have any extra money to have the business cards and stationery reprinted. As the years rolled on and my business struggled, and I had now become a born-again believer myself, I felt the Holy Spirit convicting me to get rid of that number.

But I still balked at the prospect of losing business. I finally decided to get another phone number in addition to the 666 number and had new cards and stationery printed with both numbers on them. As I handed out the business cards over the next several years, I felt everyone would now have my new number as I listed it first. But I still wasn't ready to totally step out in faith, even though, after several years, about 90 percent of my customers now had my new number.

The company still continued to struggle for about another four years with no significant gain in sales. The thought continued to plague me that I probably should drop that number, but I resisted. I started to consider closing down the company for lack of business, but instead, I decided to step out in faith and cancel the 666 number as the Holy Spirit continued to press me on this issue. I finally called the phone company and canceled that number. And within weeks, orders started pouring in from companies that I had quoted previously but had never gotten a sale. In addition, I received calls asking me to quote machinery from companies that I had never called on or even heard of. To this day, I still don't know how they got my phone number. But they too placed large orders with me from as far away from Ohio as New York. Whereas before I was quoting machine tools below my competition and still not receiving the orders, I was now getting orders where I was not even the low quote. My annual sales for the remaining two years were the best in my business career, approximately five or six times annually compared to my previous sixteen years of business. In those final two years, I had done nothing different in terms of frequency of sales calls or advertising. And the economy, both locally and nationally, was no different than in the preceding years. One customer in our area, whom I had quoted hundreds of times with not a single sale, was now giving me most of their machine tool business. In retrospect, I wish I had listened to the Lord years before.

It was hard for me to turn over control of my business life to God, as I think it is very hard for most of us to relinquish complete control of our lives to Him. As I have over the years been able to let go of certain areas of my life, I have still found it hard to give total control to the Lord. But that is exactly what God calls us to do. One of the best illustrations I can think of, that I heard many years later from a young man in our church youth group was from a sermon he gave to our congregation on Youth Sunday. He brought in a bowl of M&M's and showed how we are willing to give up the red M&M's and the green M&M's and the orange M&M's but not the brown M&M's. Relating this to our lives, we may be willing to give up certain areas of our life but refuse to give up others, as I did with my business. This struggle continues throughout our entire life, and we can't do it in our own strength. We daily have to rely on the Holy Spirit, who is Jesus living within us once we become believers, to convict us of the areas that we need to let go of and give us the strength we need to do so.

Giving total control over to God can take many forms. One area that I think we all struggle with is prioritizing our time and putting others ahead of ourselves. After keeping God first and foremost in our life, our next priority should be our spouse, then our children (immediate family), then monetarily providing for our family, and then church, friends, hobbies, etc. after that. When we get those priorities out of order, we are not relinquishing control of our life to God and will miss out on God's best for us, at the very least. Worst-case scenario, this could be catastrophic for our marriage and children. I have found over the years that many men and women have prioritized their work over spending quality time with their spouses or children. I once read in a book that after climbing the corporate ladder, you may find out that you were climbing the wrong ladder! The pressures at work from our bosses and business dealings can lead us away from prioritizing our relationship with God, our spouse, and then our children, ahead of our work. This is a very real struggle when trying to provide for your family and one that requires a great deal of prayer, as well as compromise and understanding between husband and wife. This is made even more difficult in our secular society that doesn't really value marriage or family and places such a high priority on material possessions and status.

My area of weakness was not putting my work first; rather it was putting my children ahead of my wife. This seems to be even more prevalent among women than it is among men. When both parents put the children first, this often leads to two strangers staring across the table when the kids leave home. We need to be very intentional about keeping the relationship with our spouse strong throughout the years. This is where a weekly date night can really be beneficial. My wife and I stumbled upon the benefits of spending this quality time together each week strictly by God's grace. I wanted to practice sailboat racing starts without the distraction of our children. Every Wednesday night during the summer months we would get a babysitter and head to the boat to practice for the upcoming races. In addition to working on our sailboat racing, we found it gave us the time we needed to communicate with one another and work on resolving any differences. We found those date nights helped us draw closer to one another and become more in agreement with one another regarding child-rearing, discipline, and finances, etc. We made a pledge to each other to keep that night sacred and not schedule anything else on Wednesday nights. Before the date nights, we didn't take the time to communicate our thoughts and feelings to each other on a regular basis, which was one thing that was taking a toll on our marriage. Because these weekly date nights started us on a much better path of communication, we decided to continue them throughout the year and we continued this practice from the time our boys were very small through their junior high years when we could no longer leave them with a babysitter.

Years after we started our date nights, we attended a weekend marriage seminar where we heard them emphasize the importance of regular date nights. And it wasn't until even later in our marriage, when we started doing marriage mentoring for our church, that we really learned even better communication and conflict resolution skills. Because children and their schedules can be so demanding, it leaves little time for parents to communicate and build a truly intimate relationship. As parents, we think that we are doing what is best in meeting our children's needs, but, according to God's order of things, by not putting our spouse second behind our relationship with the Lord, which should always be first, we are really being disobedient. It is so easy (and destructive) to take our relationship with our spouse for granted. Dr. James Dobson, who started Focus on the Family, said, "The best gift a father can give his children is to love their mother." And obviously, the reverse is true as well. The greatest gift a mother can give her children is to love their father.

Another area where many men struggle is prioritizing their hobbies over their relationship with God and their families. This can include golf, fishing, hunting, watching TV, etc. While these are all great hobbies, it is a challenge to keep them from becoming too dominant in our life. The more you can include your spouse and children in these hobbies, the better off your family will be. We found boating to be a great family sport, and it helped keep our family close, even into our sons' college years. If your entire family enjoys a sport, such as golf, fishing, skiing, these too can help build a strong family. Our oldest son, Bill, called it "Bonding with the fam!" You may not always feel like doing this. God's way is always the harder path to take. You may want to spend more time at work or playing golf with your buddies or watching TV or shopping instead of helping or spending time with your spouse or children, but in essence, you are being disobedient by not giving control of that area of your life over to God. We are all guilty at times of this sin because we are all basically self-centered. These are all areas of my life where I have struggled. With the Lord's help, I feel that I have grown spiritually but still have a long way to go. None of us can ever say that we have arrived. We are all a work in progress.

CHAPTER 3

Prayer and Fasting

As I said in chapter 1, my mother taught me to pray at a very early age. It was a simple, rote bedtime prayer, but it must have made an impression on me. Throughout my life, even though I didn't know Jesus as my Lord and Savior or really very much about Him at all, I continued to pray when I felt that I needed God's help. Most of the time, like most people, I only prayed as a last resort or when I desperately wanted something. I treated God as more of a cosmic Santa Claus, rather than how we should treat Him as our loving Father and best friend, who wants to have frequent conversations with us.

As we seldom went to church and never prayed before meals, I rarely experienced people praying to God. In my teen years, when I was on the high school football team, we had a team chaplain who would pray with us before games. In that prayer, the chaplain would ask the Lord to watch over us and protect us from injury. Since I did see my fellow players get injured and I myself was injured during a game my senior year, I really didn't give much thought to praying and possibly even doubted the effectiveness of prayer. Since I had never read the Bible at this point in my life, I wasn't familiar with any of God's promises. It is only looking back over the years that I can see God's hand on my life, even before I really knew Him. After graduating from high school, I think the only times I prayed were when I was concerned about my health or when I wanted to get admitted to Kent State University to complete my college education after flunking out of Ohio State.

I hate to admit it, but prayer didn't really become a significant part of my life until I was in my midforties. I realize now how central prayer needs to be in the life of a believer. My prayer life really started to become more regular when our oldest son, Bill, got his driver's license and started becoming more independent from us. The road to and from the high school was very narrow and treacherous, and numerous teenagers had lost their lives on that stretch of road. In addition, he started making the two-and-a-half-hour drive to Lake Erie and back during the summers with his younger brother in the car, and we were obviously very concerned for their safety. At about that same time we joined a couples' small group Bible study where we went around the room with our prayer requests, and I witnessed many prayers answered during those years. While we will never know why some prayers are answered and others are not, we have to trust that God knows the bigger picture and He has a plan to "work all things together for good."

The greatest answers to prayer came during the time when we put our house on the market in Ohio after our younger son, John, graduated from high school, hoping to make the move to Florida. I had always wanted to move to Florida after our boys were both out of high school, and I had shared with many people that that was my dream. I had found this small town in Southwest Florida with canals where you could have your boat behind your house and which led out to the Intracoastal Waterway (ICW) and the Gulf of Mexico. Punta Gorda was a sleepy little fishing town with approximately sixteen thousand people, about the size of the town I had grown up in, with approximately fifty miles of canals. It was an ideal boating community and more affordable for us than most other coastal locations in Florida. I had found Punta Gorda many years before this when our boys were still small but didn't want to move them away from grandparents, have to change job location, and disrupt their schooling. Being a boater, this was truly a dream-come-true location, but first, we had to sell the house in Ohio. I had only told my brother and sister about Punta Gorda over the years because I wanted to keep it a secret so that the prices wouldn't go up to where we couldn't afford to make the move. Unfortunately, about two years before our son John graduated, I got a call from my sister saying that Punta Gorda had been named the second-best place in the country to live and the best place in the south by *Money* magazine.

Even though moving to Florida was my heart's desire, I wanted to make sure that this was God's will for us. As my wife and I discussed the situation, we realized that we could make this happen by simply selling the house at below market value, so we needed some kind of reassurance that we were in the center of God's will with this move. This was such a big decision for us, leaving behind my father and brother and the house where we had raised our sons for the past twenty-one years. Plus, both of our sons were in college in Indiana. We called in three realtors to establish a realistic market value or selling price. Although putting out a fleece to the Lord is not biblically grounded, we decided to put a value on the house below which we would not go. If the house did not sell for that amount, we felt that would be a sign from the Lord that we should stay in Ohio. So in August 1997, we signed a six-month contract with a realtor who was highly regarded in the area. Within a month we received an offer on the house that was $20,000 below our fleece. We turned down the offer, which angered the agent who accused us of not really wanting to sell our house. They proceeded to tell us that we would never sell the house at that price. We asked them to please keep on showing the house, but for four months the house was never shown again. When their contract ran out in January 1998, we called in another realtor who told us that he thought he could meet or exceed our desired selling price (i.e., our fleece, which we did not disclose to either agent). We signed another six-month contract and made the decision that, if it did not sell within that period, we would take the house off the market and stay in Ohio. This would be our sign from the Lord that He didn't want us to move to Florida.

I had closed down my machine tool sales business when we first put the house on the market, so I was free at that point to travel. My wife and I decided that right after the New Year we would head to Punta Gorda, where we had committed to a two-and-a-half-month lease. Our intent was to buy a fixer-upper in the town next door, rehab it while we were in Florida, and flip it to make some money. Because of *Money* magazine, home prices in the area were rising and flipping homes was becoming popular.

Over Christmas our younger son, John, had surgery to remove what they thought was just a sebaceous cyst on his calf that was pressing on a nerve and causing him pain. After New Year's John headed back to college, and we loaded up the van with our luggage and tools and headed to Florida, not thinking to wait for the pathology report. God, however, had other plans in mind. Proverbs 19:21 says, "Many are the plans in a person's heart, but it is the Lord's purpose that prevails." We were only there a couple of days when we got a call from my sister-in-law in Ohio that we needed to contact John's surgeon right away. She gave us his phone number to call him at home that night. He broke the news to us that John had a very rare form of cancer that he had never seen in his career but had studied about it in medical school. He, fortunately, knew the name of a surgeon who specialized in that particular cancer and fortunately operated out of Akron General Hospital in Ohio. We contacted that surgeon the next morning, and he conveyed to us that he needed to operate as soon as possible in order to get clean margins and prevent any further spread. He said that it could not wait until John's spring break.

One of the hardest things we have ever had to do was to call our freshman son at college and tell him that he had cancer and that we were driving the seventeen hours to pick him up in Indiana and drive him another six hours to Akron for the surgery. It was a time of intense prayer, but my wife and I both had peace about it, especially since the surgeon had said that this cancer usually did not spread rapidly. After the second surgery and taking John back to school, we made the decision to stay in Ohio for a couple of weeks until we received the pathology report. We were grateful to the Lord that the report came back that they had gotten clean margins and that he didn't need any further treatment.

Unfortunately, our original plan to rehab a house was now totally unrealistic due to time restraints. Since we could not get our money back on the rental, we decided to head back down to Florida and look at homes for sale, even though our house in Ohio still had not sold. With the shortened time frame, we took the opportunity to get to know the area and look at both existing homes and home builders. We quickly realized that we really couldn't afford a new home with the money we hoped to get out of the sale of our house in Ohio. We looked at three existing homes that were in our price range but were told that they would be gone in the next few weeks if our house in Ohio didn't sell soon. So as a backup plan, we decided to look at lots for sale, figuring we could easily resell a lot if our home in Ohio didn't sell for the amount of our fleece.

The next series of events could only be described as miraculous. And I really realized just how miraculous they were some years later, as God knows the future and we don't. When you put control of your life in God's hands, it is amazing how He works everything out. We found two lots that were out of our price range by about $10,000. I called about the one that was for sale by the owner, who proceeded to ask me a number of questions about me and my family. I answered some of his questions and told him that our sons were in college in Indiana. I then asked him, out of curiosity, why he wanted all of this information. He informed me that he was from Indiana, that he owned the two adjoining lots and was planning on building on the one, and thus we would be his neighbor. He said that he would sell the lot to us, and in the course of the conversation, he asked if we had found a builder, to which I replied, "Not one that we can afford!"

He told us of a reputable builder who he was planning on using and who would be $20,000 lower than any of the other quotes that we had received. We decided to check out his builder, who we hadn't heard of because he was located in the adjacent town. When we walked into their model, it turned out to be exactly the floor plan that we wanted. And when we sat down with the sales rep, who was incredibly kind to work with, he confirmed to us that we could indeed build this house for $20,000 less than our previous quotes, getting us closer to our price range. The other lot that we were considering was selling for the same price and was closer to the harbor by boat, was within walking distance to downtown, and was not on nearly as busy a street. It was also on the same canal as a good friend of ours from Ohio. But it was still $10,000 too high for us to stay within our budget! We were within days of heading back to Ohio when we visited the realtor we had been working with, and much to our amazement, the price on the second lot, that we actually liked better, had just been reduced by $10,000 by the owner. While the owner of the first lot refused to negotiate the price, the owner of the second one had owned his lot for ten years and had just made the decision to lower the price to get rid of it. So we signed the contract on the lot the day before we left to go back to Ohio. We now owned a lot to build on and had a builder all lined up with the floor plan we wanted, all within our budget, should our house in Ohio sell for the price of our fleece. Only God could have accomplished that! We later learned that the person who would become our next-door neighbor was a Christian lady from Ohio who had been praying for years for Christian neighbors to build next to her.

Fast-forward to the summer and our house in Ohio still had not sold. We grew tired of staying home, waiting for a possible showing, so we decided to trailer our boat up to Lake Erie and stay on it for a month. If our house wasn't sold by the time we got back, our contract with the second realtor would be expiring and we had made the decision to take the house off the market and stay in Ohio. We were just pulling the boat out of the water to trailer it home when we got a call from our realtor that he had an offer on the house that well exceeded our fleece. We could hardly believe the great news! We got home, signed the contract, and started preparing to make the move to Florida on October 1. We contacted the builder and signed the contract with him in order to get on his construction schedule. He promised us that the house would be done in seven months, but it was actually completed in six months and under budget.

When we moved here, we began searching for a church. We tried a number of different denominations, but we felt the Lord calling us to the First United Methodist Church in Punta Gorda, which was within walking distance of our house. We felt led to attend there for a variety of reasons. They had a prayer group, which my wife was looking for; small groups, which we both wanted; and a Vacation Bible School that was very similar to what we had had in Ohio. We were at the church about seven months when the youth director put out a plea for volunteers for his annual trip to Disney's Night of Joy. Since we were having a really bad case of "empty-nest syndrome" at the time, being away from our two sons, we decided to volunteer. He needed drivers and chaperones for that trip to Orlando, so we started coming to youth group on Sunday nights to get to know the teens. While it was more of just a youth center at that time, we really fell in love with the teens and started coming every Sunday night for the next two years. Be careful what you pray for because I had promised the Lord, if He got me to Florida, I would get more involved in church. There, unfortunately, was no adult Sunday school program after the contemporary service; and when we spoke to the head pastor about this, he suggested that we start one. So using a video study that we had participated in at our Sunday school class in Ohio, we began facilitating a Sunday school class here. We started out with eleven members in that class, and when we ended up getting more involved with the teens and had to turn the class over to someone else, there were still only eleven members. The gentleman who took over the class had the gift of teaching, and the class quickly grew to over forty. This obviously was not our calling!

Two years after we began volunteering on Sunday nights, the youth director laid down his keys and said he quit after a disagreement with the head pastor. Since we were the only ones who knew the teens, they asked us to serve as interim leaders until they could hire a new youth director. After about six months and no success in filling the position, I began to question whether God was actually calling me to take on this part-time position. Even before the old director had left, we had started a Bible study with any teens who were interested. Being a youth director was going to be a huge undertaking, and having had no theological training, I wasn't sure if I was capable of doing the job. Knowing that it says in Matthew 18:6 that you are not to lead a younger person astray or suffer serious consequences, I took that scripture very seriously and prayed before youth group every Sunday night that the Lord would give me the words to say to these young people. He answered my prayers, as I really felt the Lord helping me to stay a few steps ahead of the teens in our small group Bible studies and our Sunday school class.

Over the next five years, the Lord grew our youth group from fourteen to averaging about sixty-five teens on Sunday nights, with a hurricane midway through, which disrupted the program for about six months and caused some families to leave the area. The Lord also allowed us in those five years to start a small group Bible study with the teens, which started with just two girls at our house and ended up the last year with as many as twenty-five teens. God had provided us with the perfect home, with its close proximity to the church and the layout having a separate living room and family room, which allowed us to have two Bible studies going on at once. My wife taught one, and I taught the other. Little did we know when we prayed and put out a fleece for God's will to be done regarding our moving to Florida, that He had plans for our lives that we couldn't even have begun to imagine. Ephesians 3:20 says, "Now to him who is able to do immeasurably more than all we ask or imagine, according to his power that is at work within us."

During those first couple of years, my wife had joined our church's Tuesday morning prayer group. Her work schedule changed so she was no longer able to attend, so I decided to start going and ask for prayer for our youth group to grow not only in numbers but also in spiritual maturity. Week after week, they prayed for us, and the youth and I believe that God answered those prayers.

Twenty years later, we are both still active in that prayer ministry every Tuesday morning. Over those twenty years, we have seen so many prayer requests answered, both personally and for members of our church and their families. One of the reasons for the success of our church has been that this prayer group has been faithfully praying for our pastors and the ministries of the church long before we ever started attending.

My wife and I both believe in the power of prayer! This quote on the importance of prayer just came in today's devotional from the Presidential Prayer Team (isn't God amazing!):

> The Bible shows us many examples of prayer. Adam and Eve talked to God in the Garden of Eden. Abraham and God discussed God's promises of making a great nation from Abraham's lineage. Abraham's servant asked God for help to find a wife for Isaac and God led him straight to Abraham's

relatives. Moses talked to God as to a friend and led the nation of Israel out of Egypt. Joshua listened to God and did everything that God commanded.

Jonah argued with God, but God had the last word by sending a fish to swallow him. Followers of Christ prayed for Peter when he was in jail and an angel came and rescued him. Jesus talked to the Heavenly Father. He'd get off by himself and pray all night. On many occasions, He taught about prayer and how important it is and even gave His disciples a pattern with "the Lord's Prayer" (Matthew 6:5–18). In it, He taught them to acknowledge who God is, and pray for His will to be accomplished on Earth, for daily needs to be met, for forgiveness (with a forgiving heart), to be led away from temptation, and to escape evil.

Shortly after we joined the church, our pastor started an annual event in January called the Festival of Lights. During the Sunday morning services that day, each person is given a three-by-five-inch index card on which they are to write the names of lost friends and relatives (those who need to accept Jesus as their Lord and Savior) and any personal prayer requests. These cards are then placed in special boxes, one in our main sanctuary and the other in the Life Center where we hold our contemporary service. These cards are prayed over throughout the year by the Tuesday morning prayer group, along with the personal prayer request cards that are filled out weekly by our congregation. These prayer requests can range from financial to health to marital problems to family/friend reconciliation to spiritual growth or other needs, wants, or concerns.

It has been incredible over the years to witness how many of those prayer requests have been answered. We have seen prayers answered for salvation for individual's family members, for jobs, and for the reconciliation of relationships. Many of these prayers have taken years before they were answered, after much perseverance in prayer. Personally, we have seen so many prayer requests answered that we can't even begin to list them all. Some of the most significant answers to prayer were that our oldest son, Bill, recommitted his life to Christ; both of our sons married born-again Christian women; and the healthy births of our two granddaughters and two grandsons.

After Bill began dating Brooke in 2003 and they became engaged in January 2004, we began praying for a day job for Bill, who had been working as production manager at an automobile assembly plant on night shift for two years. Bill's desire since college had been to work for a boat manufacturing company. Before their September 2004 wedding, he *just happened* to see a boat manufacturing job position online for a lamination manager which required a bachelor's degree in mechanical engineering and five years of automotive production line experience, both of which he had. God answered our prayers for a day job and Bill's prayers for a boat manufacturing job in Ohio right before he was about to get married. Shortly after their marriage began, the Lord provided his wife a job at a Christian school, which again was a huge answer to prayer. After working at the boat plant for three years, he and his wife decided that they wanted to move to Florida, and the opportunity arose for Bill to transfer within the company to a plant in Florida. I will share more on his transfer to Florida in the next chapter on miracles.

No request is too small to ask the Lord. He is not too busy to hear our prayer requests and cares about even the smallest details. Nor is any request too large, if it is in line with His will. One request that we prayed for many years, not only with our church group but also on many Sunday nights on family conference calls, was for my dad's salvation. My brother and his wife, along with our niece Julie and sometimes our son Bill, prayed that my Dad would come to a saving knowledge of Christ. There was no kinder or better man than my dad, especially in how he treated others. I know there were times when Dad was treated unfairly, especially at work, but I never heard him say a bad word about anyone. He never used crude or coarse language, nor took the Lord's name in vain. He was never drunk or abusive. He was admired throughout the community by those with whom he worked, by those with whom he served on many boards, and by his neighbors and friends. He was a model husband, father, and son, taking care of his mother and my mother in the last years of their lives. No son could ask for a better father. Unfortunately, because he was such a good man, I think that he, like many people at the time, felt that he could earn his way to heaven. He had never acknowledged his need for Jesus and had only recently started attending church when he remarried after my mom's death. He accepted Christ as his Savior just three days before he died, which I will also cover in the next chapter on miracles.

While being a *prayer warrior* sounds intimidating to many, it really just means being in conversation throughout the day with our Heavenly Father, which is something we should all strive to do and so often we neglect to do. We either get so busy doing other things we deem more important or we feel like we shouldn't "bother" God with our needs and concerns. But nothing is more important than keeping that close, intimate relationship with Him. I cannot think of better prayer warriors than my wife or my mother-in-law. My mother-in-law prayed daily for our family and others, and I know her prayers were answered in the way our two sons have given their lives to Christ and are now raising their children. I also credit her prayers and the prayers of my wife's Bible study for my coming to Christ. My wife also prays daily for our family and frequently for her sister, who has a biochemical imbalance, as has our church prayer group. At the time of this writing, her sister has never been better, despite the COVID-19 pandemic.

We do not thank God enough for the trillions of things He does for us each and every day. So often we pray, but then when our prayer is answered, we fail to acknowledge God for having answered that prayer. I have failed many times to give thanks, as I should, for such things as my health, my longevity, and my wonderful family (parents, siblings, spouse, children, and grandchildren). One of the other things that I haven't mentioned yet is how thankful I am that our daughters-in-law's parents are all born-again believers and have intact marriages. I am very grateful for living in a country that allows for freedom of worship and freedom of speech. I am also so very thankful that we have food in abundance in this country when many around the world are hunting for their next meal. I thank God for the beautiful homes that He has provided for us. I thank Him for getting us to Florida. He has provided not only for our needs but many, if not all, of our wants as well. Philippians 4:19 says, "And my God will meet all your needs according to His glorious riches in Christ Jesus." Everything that we own is a gift from God. He is really the owner of it all, and we are merely stewards of what He has given us. Psalm 105:1–3 says, "Thank the Lord for all the glorious things he does, proclaim them to the nations. Sing his praises and tell everyone about his miracles. Glory in the Lord, O worshipers of God, rejoice."

While there is no right or wrong way to talk to God, I have found the acronym ACTS to be very helpful in how to give balance to our prayers. The *A* stands for adoration. Too often our prayers become just a wish list of what we want when we need to learn how to really worship God for who He is. The *C* stands for confession. This is something that I find very difficult to do, but more recently, I have been working on this. The *T* stands for thanksgiving, about which I have just elaborated. And finally, the *S* stands for supplication or making our requests known to God. This is where most of us tend to put our emphasis.

Another acronym that I just learned from our pastor and that really spoke to me is PRAY. The *P* stands for praise and thanksgiving (Psalm 136). The *R* stands for repent or asking for forgiveness (Psalm 139). The *A* stands for ask—petitions, intercessions, and praying for revival. And the *Y* stands for yield—yielding our will to the will of God for our lives.

First Corinthians 2:15–16 says, "But the spiritual man has insight into everything, and that bothers and baffles the man of the world, who can't understand him at all. How could he? For certainly he has never been one to know the Lord's thoughts, or to discuss them with Him, or to move the hands of God by prayer."

My last thought on the topic of prayer is to emphasize the importance of spending time with God daily. We can pray at any time or in any place like praying in the shower or riding in the car or while we are exercising. God wants to hear our daily needs and wants. But the best place to pray, when we are able, is to find a quiet place alone, where we can focus our thoughts solely on the Lord. As it says in Matthew 6:6, "But when you pray, go away by yourself, shut the door behind you, and pray to your Father secretly. Then your Father, who knows all secrets, will reward you." And like David, we shouldn't be afraid to express our deepest emotions to Him—our fears, our disappointments, our longings, our frustrations, and of course, our joys!

The leader of a small group that we were in also taught us about the tremendous power of praying back scripture to God. This helps ensure that we are praying in line with His will, as we repeat His very own words back to Him from the Scriptures. Let's all have the goal of becoming prayer warriors!

Fasting

Fasting has been a part of my prayer life for some time now, maybe not as much as it should have been. To my understanding, we fast because it directs our thoughts more toward God's purposes and helps us focus our thoughts on what we are praying about. Ezra 8:23 says, "We fasted and earnestly prayed that our God would take care of us, and he heard our prayer." When I fast and feel my stomach growling, it forces me to focus more and pray about the concerns I have at the time. I feel it draws me closer to the Lord during this time.

I didn't start fasting until after my oldest son, Bill, had graduated from high school and we got a new pastor at our church. He and I would meet for breakfast on a regular basis, and we would share our struggles professionally and personally. We had a lot in common as he was also raising sons, and we became very close friends. I came under the conviction that I needed to be lifting him in prayer and decided to fast on his behalf one day a week. He was dealing with a difficult situation because of the church's debt that he had inherited and the resistance of some church members to a new pastor. I fasted for him for several years until we made the move to Florida. I was also fasting at the time for safety and guidance for our son Bill as he was facing many challenges in his college years.

Since moving to Florida and becoming involved in the Tuesday morning prayer group, I once again began to fast on Tuesday mornings for the prayer concerns of our church. I have also fasted for safety and health issues for our family and for family relationships, as well as when I have had to make major decisions. And I have fasted, as I pray, for our church leadership, asking God to give them wisdom.

Jesus taught about fasting in Matthew 6:16–18, saying that when we fast, we are not to make it obvious, drawing attention to ourselves. Matthew 6:17 says, "When you fast, put on festive clothing, so that no one will suspect you are hungry, except your Father who knows every secret. And He will reward you." Notice that Jesus didn't say *if* you fast, He said *when* you fast, so he obviously felt that fasting is something that all of His followers should do.

My main point is that, in reflecting back on my life, I have not spent enough time in prayer to such an awesome God! And I also wish I had kept a journal so I would better recall all of the many answers to prayer and fasting that I have experienced. What I have recounted here are just a few of the many answers to prayer that we have witnessed.

CHAPTER 4

Miracles

There are only two ways to live your life.
One as though nothing is a miracle. The
other is as though everything is a miracle.

—Albert Einstein

I never really thought much about miracles until we
made the decision to move to Florida and we experienced one miracle after another. But even then, I
really saw them as just answers to prayer and not
really miracles. I, like most people, probably didn't
think much about the daily miracles that are happening all around us. We tend to write things off
as mere coincidence or just take them for granted.
I think the first miracle that I actually regarded
as a miracle was the birth of our two sons, and I
wasn't even a believer at that time. But the older I
get and the more time I have to reflect, the more

I see miracles all around me on a daily basis. The whole of creation is really a miracle. The variety of plants and flowers, the abundance and variety of our food supply, the incredible number of different species of animals, fish, and birds, and the complexity of the human body are just a few of the miracles we witness every day. Think about the universe, the stars and the planets, the way the earth spins on its own axis, and its relationship to the sun, which allows it to be neither too hot nor too cold. More recently, I learned from Del Tackett on Focus on the Family's *The Truth Project* the miracle of the blood clotting mechanism in our body which prevents us from bleeding to death when we cut ourselves. The miraculous way that our body heals after a sickness, injury, or surgery is really another miracle. We tend to take God and the active role He plays in our daily lives, working miracles all around us, for granted. I am sure that I do! What an extraordinary God we serve!

I know that God has performed hundreds, if not thousands, of miracles in my life, but I would like to share a few that really stand out to me. I have to say that I consider the way my wife and I met to have been a miracle, but I am going to cover that story in another chapter. And I have already mentioned in the previous chapter on prayer how we came about getting our home in Florida, which truly was also a miracle.

Let me start off here with the story of how our oldest son, Bill, and his wife, Brooke, were able to make the move to Florida, nine years after we moved there. Bill had a desire from an early age to work for a boat company, and by the time he was halfway through college, he had even more clarity that was the industry he really wanted to work in. However, after seeking summer jobs and applying to almost every boat company in the industry as a graduating senior, he didn't have a single offer or even an interview in the marine industry. Bill graduated from college in 1999, taking a job as a supervisor in the automotive industry but never losing that unfulfilled desire. After five years of experience in automotive and many more closed doors, Bill was led to apply for a lamination supervisor position at a boat builder in Ohio. One of the first miracles the Lord worked in Bill's career was to fulfill his dream and in a way that only God could provide. The boat company contacted Bill about his application, but instead of accepting his application for a supervisor position, they wanted to pursue Bill as a candidate for a manager position because of his strong experience in automotive. God had used what was a disappointment early in Bill's career for his ultimate good, and that continued many times in miraculous ways as Bill's career progressed.

After three years of enjoying his job as assembly manager at the boat company in Ohio, he and Brooke began to desire to get away from Ohio's winters. Again, God was at work. Bill happened to see and apply for an assembly manager opening at a boat plant on Florida's east coast. Even though it would be a lateral move within the company, it would at least get them to Florida. At about the same time he was given the opportunity through the company to take a Lean Six Sigma course, which he had always wanted to take at his former job but was never given the opportunity. As I understand it, Lean Six Sigma is a quality assurance program developed by General Electric. This course proved to be life-changing for Bill and Brooke. There, in green belt training, the instructor took an immediate liking to Bill. As they got to know each other better during that week, Bill shared with him his desire to move to Florida and that he had applied for a job. It turned out that the instructor had worked at that plant and suggested to Bill that he come to work for him instead of at another boat plant in Florida. Bill expressed his concern that he was now just working on his green belt certification and would need to have his black belt in order to qualify for that position. The instructor told him that he needed someone with Bill's knowledge of boat building and that he could teach him the rest. He reassured him that within a short period of time, he would have the necessary certification. Bill and Brooke felt the Lord leading them away from Ohio, and after the interview process, Bill was offered the role of Lean Six Sigma manager in Florida.

The many miracles of this move included the timing of the training, the desire to look for another opportunity, the unity of the decision in their marriage, and that the move was paid for by the company. They had purchased an older home in Ohio which they needed to sell in order to make the move. The economy in their area was becoming more depressed at the time because of many plant closings, which represented the loss of hundreds of jobs. But again, miraculously, the Lord caused their home to be sold within a few months for a profit and also included an additional selling bonus from the relocation company. And if all that were not enough, approximately six months after they made the move to Florida, the boat plant in Ohio, where Bill had been working, was shut down completely and moved to North Carolina. If he had not taken the new job in Florida, he would have been unemployed. Looking back, we all could see how God had performed a miracle on their behalf in the timing of this move.

The Lord went on to perform many more miracles in Bill's career as He sustained their family in Florida through the recession of 2008 while continuing to bless Bill with roles that were greater than anything Bill could have dreamed of during his college years.

The next miracle I would like to share is how my dad came to salvation just days before he died. As I previously mentioned, my father was a wonderful man; but because of some negative experiences regarding church in his youth, he really felt that most Christians were hypocrites. He was able to live in his own home right up to the time of his death, and God had placed a wonderful young Christian couple, Evie and Todd, right across the street from him. After suffering a stroke, he could no longer prepare his own meals and at times also needed some supervision. Our family ended up hiring Evie to bring him his evening meal. Todd, who was a physical therapist, also came over frequently in the evening to help Dad get ready for bed. Over several years, they developed a close and trusting relationship. I had visited my dad in September 2009, and seeing him then made me think that this would probably be our last time together, as he looked very weak and frail. It was a very emotional goodbye for all of us. I was able to tell my dad at that time how much I loved him and that he deserved a better son than I had been to him. As we left him, I was deeply concerned about his salvation. Right after a Thanksgiving visit that year from my sister and her husband, who live in California, my dad ended up in the hospital. Evie expressed to Todd that she didn't think that Dad would be coming back home this time and encouraged Todd to go and pray with him at the hospital. Through Gary Smalley's book *The Five Love Languages*, we had come to realize that Dad's primary love language was gifts as he always loved giving and receiving gifts. Todd, however, was unaware of this, but through the prompting of the Holy Spirit, he shared with Dad that the good news of the gospel is really a gift that we have to not only receive but personally open. He asked my dad if he could pray the prayer of salvation with him to receive the gift of eternal life through Jesus, which he did. Two days later, as the hospital was preparing to discharge him to an assisted living facility, with my sister-in-law Sandy sitting by his side, my dad quietly and unexpectedly passed away. What a miracle, a blessing, and a huge comfort to me and our entire family to know that our dad would be waiting for us someday in heaven.

Another miracle that we experienced with a more earthly benefit involved my sister-in-law JoAnn, who has suffered from a debilitating biochemical imbalance since she was twenty-seven years old. She was able to live on her own until she turned sixty-two years old, at which time we helped get her placed in an assisted living facility. About three months after we had gotten her placed, we took her back to her condo to sort through more of her belongings. When she walked into her bedroom, she realized that the carpeting was soaking wet and her bedspread and pillows were covered with mildew. Apparently, a pipe in the wall had burst and flooded her apartment. We had been dreading having to rehab her condo before we could put it on the market for sale. Everything in the apartment was dated and very worn, as she had lived there for almost forty years. The kitchen and bathrooms needed to be completely remodeled, and the ceilings were that old-fashioned popcorn finish. Plus, all of the flooring needed to be replaced. We lived about three hours away, and trying to find a contractor to do the work or do it ourselves seemed like a monumental task. Our only other option was to sell it *as is*, which would have netted her a lot less money that she now needed for her care. So the flood actually turned out to be a blessing in disguise. We contacted her insurance company, who sent in a mold remediation company, which took the interior walls completely down to the studs and removed all of the kitchen cabinets and vanities. After we got the report back that the mold was completely removed, they recommended a contractor to do the rehab work. Unfortunately at this point, things got a little more difficult as his prices were way out of line. But God was totally in control, and He led us to some of JoAnn's neighbors who had just remodeled their condo. They highly recommended their contractor, who *just happened* to live in the same complex, directly across the parking lot from JoAnn's condo. He was fabulous to work with and actually came in below what the insurance company had given us for the remodeling work, while the other contractor had been well above that figure. It took about nine months for the work to be completed, but during that time, the demand for condos had increased significantly; thus, the price we were able to sell her condo for was much higher. So thanks to the Lord, we were able to get her condo remodeled at no cost to her and sold for close to double what she had previously been offered. God is good, all the time!

It is often difficult in the middle of trying circumstances to see how God is working miracles on our behalf. One such experience happened early in my Christian walk when I lost my business partner and dear friend very unexpectedly to a massive heart attack. He had been my boss and mentor in the years before I went back to college. He also helped me through college by providing me with summer jobs, and many years later, when I decided to start my own business, he helped me to get established. While we each independently owned our own machine tool sales companies, we had decided to start another company jointly to purchase new and used machine tools, mostly at auction, which required more capital than was available to us individually. Therefore at the time of his death, we jointly owned a great deal of machinery and had leased office space together. We had our machinery warehoused in a building in the Bolivar Industrial Park that I, along with two other investors, owned. I was in the process of building another industrial building just down the road to warehouse our machinery because half of the one I owned had been leased to a local job shop with an option to buy and the job shop owner needed the entire building and wanted to exercise his option.

The new warehouse was almost complete when my partner passed away. I was now in a very difficult financial situation, having to liquidate all of our machinery to help settle his estate and also having lost any income from his renting space in the new building. I, fortunately, was able to liquidate all of our machinery and pay off my partner's widow and get out of the lease on our office space. But now I was faced with an empty industrial building with no rental income coming in and no used machinery to sell. Incredibly, shortly after liquidating our machinery and without my even having advertised that I had space for rent, a gentleman who owned a gum label company was looking for more space and approached me about renting the building with an option to buy. Despite the difficult circumstances I found myself in, I have learned through the years that God is definitely a "last-minute God" and His timing is always perfect. Praise His holy name!

Another example of God working a miracle in my life occurred about four years ago when I, unfortunately, developed a very large herniated disc between my L4 and L5 (lower back) vertebrae. I wasn't able to straighten up and was in excruciating pain. I wanted to avoid surgery at all costs as I had heard too many stories of failed back surgeries. My family doctor gave me a cortisone shot and oral prednisone, which helped relieve the pain temporarily. But feeling better, I overdid and ended up in worse pain than before. He sent me to have an MRI right before Christmas and referred me to a pain management specialist. I had one appointment to see the pain doctor before Christmas, and he then scheduled the procedure for immediately after Christmas. Unfortunately the morning of the procedure I got a call from his office saying that for personal reasons he had decided to close his practice for good beginning that day! Being in unrelenting pain, I was desperate to get relief. I called the only other pain management practice in our area and was informed that they had no openings for several weeks for their initial exam and that it would then be another week before they could do the procedure.

The following day, my wife went to our church's weekly prayer group and asked for prayer for my back and explained the situation to them. Our associate pastor said that he was very good friends with one of the pain doctors and that he would put a call into him to see what he could do. Praise God he was able to get me in to see him the very next day! After completing his initial exam, he asked me if I would like to get the shot right then, which of course I agreed to. Members of our church prayer group came over and laid hands on me and prayed. The following day I also received a phone call from a retired pastor friend who prayed for my healing over the phone. I actually felt God's healing touch during his call and immediately started to feel less pain. This time, I was very cautious not to overdo and tried to rest my back for the next six weeks. I did not want a reoccurrence or a second shot.

Later when I went for physical therapy, the therapist said, after reviewing my MRI, that it was the largest herniated disc that he had ever seen. It was a miracle that our pastor was good friends with the pain doctor and that he was willing to work me in so quickly. And it was a miracle that God answered so many prayers for my healing. To this day, I still can't stand for more than a few minutes; otherwise, I am able to walk, run, dance, and even play golf.

The severe back pain I had experienced became the impetus for us to put our 1986 36' powerboat up for sale. Because it was a flybridge, we were unable to get it under the bridge on the canal leading to our house. It was really more boat than we needed or wanted, and it was costing us a lot of money to keep it at a local marina and have the bottom cleaned monthly. It was also becoming a lot of effort for us at our age to load up the car with food and clothes and haul it down to the marina and then haul it all from the car down the long dock to the boat. I wasn't really sure that I was ready to give up boating yet but decided to leave the future up to the Lord. I had made a promise to my wife that we would get out of boating if this boat didn't sell by January 31 of the following year, as she really wanted to do some traveling. It says in Galatians 3:15 (NLT), "Dear brothers, even in everyday life a promise made by one man to another, if it is written down and signed, cannot be changed. He cannot decide afterward to do something else instead." Even though this wasn't a signed promise, I nevertheless had made a promise to my wife that I wanted to honor. We knew this would be a difficult boat to sell because of its age and the fact that banks will not lend money on a boat that old. It would have to be a cash deal, and anyone with that kind of money would most likely use it as a down payment on a much newer boat. Getting insurance was also going to be very difficult to secure.

We had a couple of showings, but after ten months, by the end of December, we still did not have an offer on the boat. In late December I received a call from a gentleman who was interested but wanted to see three other boats first. He said that he would call me back if those boats didn't work out. Several weeks later, we showed the boat to a family who was very interested and said they wanted the boat. They needed, however, to try to get financing, even though I had told them that financing would be difficult, if not impossible, to obtain. They came back the following week to take a second look at the boat with more of their family members and made an offer of $2,000 below what we were willing to accept. They were still struggling with trying to find financing and wanted a marine survey done to justify the price that we were asking. They also wanted us to haul the boat out of the water to have the surveyor examine the bottom and a marine mechanic to survey the engines and go out with them on a sea trial, all of which would have taken more than another month. Getting a boat to the local marina to be hauled out in January was also going to be very difficult due to the low water that time of year. I had told them, as I had told others, that the first one in with the money would get the boat. Because they had not located a marine surveyor and had not yet signed a contract on the boat and put down a deposit, we were still able to show the boat to others.

On Friday, January 26, I received a callback from the gentleman who had called at the end of December. The three boats that he had wanted to see first had all failed their marine surveys. He asked if he could see the boat that day, and we made arrangements to meet him and his wife at the boat at eleven in the morning. They fell in love with the boat as soon as they saw it. He didn't even ask me to start the engines and made us an acceptable offer, saying that he wanted to close on the boat that afternoon, if possible. Our mechanic turned out to be the same mechanic that he always used; so as a result, he was willing to waive the haul out, the hull and engine marine surveys, and the sea trial. He said that he had never done this on any other boat he had purchased previously. We were unable to arrange a closing on that day, but he gave us the 10 percent down payment and we scheduled the closing for the following Monday, January 29. It even turned out that his bank was also our bank, so we met there for the closing.

God had sold the boat before January 31, so Elise took this as a sign that the Lord wanted us to continue boating for a little while longer, which we have been able to do. The true miracle here was that we were even able to sell our boat for a reasonable price and without having a marine and engine survey and haul out, all of which are usually required by the buyer. We know a number of people who, unfortunately, are having difficulty selling boats of that age, and at the time of this writing, our old boat is back on the market and has been for well over a year. We want to give God the glory for His incredible kindness toward us, even in a relatively unimportant matter such as this, especially when we consider the whole scheme of things. God does care about the big and small things in our life, and our purpose in life should be to bring Him praise and glory in all things.

We have also witnessed miracles in people outside of our family. This last miracle that I want to share with you could be categorized as both a miracle and a true answer to prayer. The mother of one of our teens was stricken with a urinary tract infection. Unfortunately, she experienced a serious and very rare allergic reaction to the antibiotic that she was given and ended up being paralyzed from the waist down. She was told by her physician that she might never walk again. Our church prayer group was contacted about her condition; and in a very rare occurrence, our two pastors and several from the prayer group, including myself and my wife, drove to her house to lay hands on her. Our pastor anointed her with oil as we prayed over her. Miraculously, within a relatively short period of time, she was up walking and eventually was able to return to church without the assistance of a cane or a walker.

These represent just a few of the many miracles that I have witnessed over the years, both within our family and our church family. There would be far too many to share in this chapter. Seeing life with the eyes of faith makes us more aware of the miracles that God is performing all around us, which so many people attribute to mere coincidence or fate.

My hope is that anyone reading this book will start to recognize and appreciate the miracles that God is working in their lives. Miracles abound, and God loves each one of us more than we can ever truly comprehend.

CHAPTER 5

God's Guiding Hand

I know that God was watching over my life long before I knew Him personally. But it is only in retrospect that we can see how He is guiding and directing us through the people he places in our path, the choices that we make, and the failures or hardships we may encounter.

I would like to start with telling of the series of events that over the years ultimately led to meeting my wife and eventually changing most of my family's eternal destination. The best day of my life was the day my wife, Elise, and I were married. But how I got there is a long and convoluted story. From the time I was very young, I was always *in love with love*! I think that is typical of a lot of young people, as Elise says that she was very much the same way. Over the years, I liked many girls, but they didn't like me back. In junior high and high school I had a few crushes, but the feelings were never reciprocated. In the spring of my junior year, I started dating a girl named Suzy, who lived nearby, and we frequently walked home together from school. She was more than just a friend, but I can't say that I was really *in love* with her. We hung out a lot at her house and went to many dances together, such as sock hops and sweater hops, where you wore matching socks or sweaters. Because she was two years younger than me, I wasn't allowed, however, to take her to my junior or senior proms or the post-proms. I didn't really want to go to either prom without her, but my mother and my friends convinced me that I shouldn't miss out on the experience of prom and post-prom. My junior year prom date was a disaster, so I really wasn't sure if I wanted to go to my senior prom.

About six weeks before my senior prom, which was held in late April, I still had not asked anyone. At the high schools in our area, normally everyone had their dates by the end of January. My friend Tom told me about Betty, a junior girl, who was also dating someone she couldn't take to the prom or post-prom because he had already graduated from high school. She had told my friend Tom that she would like me to ask her to the prom. I had met Betty and had gotten to know her when I got injured in football because we would meet in the chiropractor's office waiting room several times a week for therapy. She was a cheerleader and had injured her back. She agreed to go with me to the prom, post-prom, and breakfast and horseback riding the next day; and we had a fabulous time. This experience changed my feelings for Suzy, and I decided to try dating some other people, especially since Suzy was gone all summer with her family camping.

Several weeks after prom, I was participating in a track meet, which was held at our neighboring rival high school. Our team won first place for the 880 relay of which I was a part, and the awards were handed out by that school's cheerleaders. My award was given to me by a cheerleader named Janet, with whom I quickly became very smitten. I have to admit, while it was pretty immature, I chased her for seven years without ever even getting a date with her. She was also, like Suzy, two years younger than me, and I tried to frequent the places where I thought she would be. While I was off to Ohio State University that fall, not knowing what I wanted to do with my life other than play football, she was still in high school. Not having a lot of direction in my life at the time, changing my major five times my freshman year, and being very homesick, my primary purpose for being at Ohio State was to try to play football. Because of high blood pressure, I wasn't able to play;

and lacking the necessary desire and study habits to be a success in college, as a result, I flunked out of the university after my freshman year. During those years, there were more students accepted into state colleges than they could accommodate, so it was very common for freshman and sophomores to not make it through to graduation. During freshman orientation, the presenter even said to us, "Look to your left and look to your right, two out of the three of you won't make it through the next four years!" In addition to poor study habits, I also was a very slow reader, possibly even dyslexic.

After completing my freshman year, I went back home and took a summer job at the highway department. Since I wasn't able to go back to Ohio State for the next two quarters due to the university's rules, that summer job lasted through the fall and winter. It was there where I met the father of the second man who helped lead me to the Lord, as I shared in my testimony. When I went back to Ohio State in the spring, my grades still weren't sufficient for me to continue, and so I didn't think a college degree was in my future.

The following summer, I took a job at my dad's place of employment, and it was there that I met a friend of my dad who offered me a job selling machine tools. He was starting a new company in

Cleveland, Ohio, and needed a salesman to cover the northeastern part of the state. After working for him for about a year and a half, I realized that this was a job that I could envision becoming a career. By this time Janet had graduated from high school and was attending Kent State University. Now that I finally realized what I wanted to do with my life, I thought it would be advantageous to have a college degree. Plus, I had promised my grandmother on her death bed that I would try one more time. So I decided to apply to Kent State University, which would get me in closer contact with Janet. I took the admission test for Kent State and wasn't able to pass it. As a result, the university admissions counselor, Mrs. Orr, required that I take two night classes before she could admit me, one being speed-reading and the other being one of my choice. I was able to take both classes at Case Western Reserve, which is in a very rough section of Cleveland, and I needed to get at least a *B* in both of them. After completing both courses, with an *A* in drafting and a *B* in speed-reading, I was finally accepted to Kent State. Over the years on campus, I tried asking Janet out several times, but by then she was in a serious relationship with a Naval Academy student. Probably the main reason that I went back to college was because of her, as I could have had a career as a machine tool salesman without a college degree. She graduated a year ahead of me and moved out of state. I never saw her again.

After graduating from Kent State with a degree in business administration, majoring in marketing, I sought out a special apprenticeship with Warner & Swasey, which was only open to college graduates. Warner & Swasey was the third largest machine tool company in the world at that time. While flunking out of college certainly wasn't something I would have hoped for or was proud of and never getting a date with "the girl of my dreams" was depressing, I realize now that God was working "all things together for my good." "We are assured and know that [God being a partner in their labor] all things work together and are [fitting into a plan] for good to and for those who love God and are called according to [His] design and purpose" (Romans 8:28 AMP). Even though I didn't know or love the Lord at that time, He knew that one day I would.

Although there were no openings in the apprentice program when I applied, they told me that because of my two years of experience in machine tool sales, they would create an opening for me. While the apprenticeship was usually a year long, I was able to complete the program in nine months, again due to my previous machine tool sales experience. This put me in line for a sales opening covering the whole state of Michigan. For the first two years, I basically lived in motels as I traveled around the state and had no permanent residence. It was a very lonely time in my life! On my parents' and the company's urging, I chose to get an apartment in Ann Arbor, Michigan, because of the University of Michigan being there and, hopefully, the opportunity to meet someone. It was also an ideal location for covering my sales territory.

My parents, after visiting the area, suggested the apartment complex I chose, but it was God who placed me in a building with twelve apartments, ten of them occupied by other singles and one by a married couple. Several times a week, whoever was available, including George and Rosemary, the married couple, would meet for dinner and conversation at Kenny's apartment. Kenny loved to cook, and we all chipped in to provide some of the food. We probably met twice a week for close to two years. The group also hung out almost every weekend together, watching sports or sitting around the community pool. I, on the other hand, would drive home to Ohio every weekend, as I had done the previous two years, especially in the summer because I had recently purchased a sailboat.

One evening, when we were gathered together at Kenny's, Rosemary asked me what it would take to keep me in Ann Arbor over the weekend. I replied, "An attractive blonde!" It turned out that Rosemary was one of the instructors in my wife's dietetic internship program at the University of Michigan. And my wife was the only unmarried blonde in the program. Rosemary was delighted at the opportunity to try to play matchmaker, so she approached Elise one day and asked if she could speak to her privately in her office. Elise was terrified that she had done something wrong! But Rosemary proceeded to ask if she could ask her a personal question. She asked Elise if she was dating anyone. When Elise replied no, Rosemary asked her if she would be willing to go out on a blind date with me. Elise said yes, and so Rosemary gave me Elise's phone number, after which I called and asked her out on our first date.

I made arrangements to pick her up at her apartment to take her ice skating at a nearby outdoor ice rink. Afterward, we met George and Rose at one of the pubs on campus. The date did not go that well for either one of us as Elise thought that I was showing off on the ice and I was unhappy to hear that she was finishing her internship in less than two months. She was planning on trying to secure a dietitian's job at a hospital in Boston. But I still decided to give it one more try, as neither one of us really got to know each other that first night, so I called her up on the spur of the moment and asked her to have dinner with me at the Gandy Dancer, the old railroad station that was then one of the finest dining spots in the area. I had not made reservations, so we ended up sitting and talking for a long time at the upstairs bar while we waited for our table. That night turned things around for Elise, as we got to know each other better and shared our future hopes and dreams. She remembers thinking that night that she could see herself married to me. I, on the other hand, still wasn't sure if I wanted to get involved any further with someone who was leaving in just a couple of months. Elise then had to fly home to Milwaukee because her father was very sick with pneumonia.

When she got back to Ann Arbor and hadn't heard from me in the interim, she approached Rosemary and said that she really wanted to go out with me again. Despite my reservations, I decided to call her for another date, and after that, we were inseparable. The next month I decided to take her home to meet my family and convinced her to try to apply for a job at Ohio State University Hospital, as she really wanted a job at a teaching hospital and there were no openings in Ann Arbor. God provided an opening at Ohio State, which was only two and half hours from Ann Arbor, which she took and ended up sharing an apartment with my sister in Columbus. One of the things that I have learned about God through the years is that He is a last-minute God. I had pretty much given up hope of finding a wife, as by now I was in my late twenties. And here I meet a woman who was only going to be in the area for less than two months. And the job at Ohio State only became available a few months after Elise graduated from her internship. But it was all part of God's incredible plan for our lives and how it would all eventually lead us into a close walk with Him.

After she started working, we would meet on the weekends at my parents' home, and that was when I taught her how to sail at a nearby inland lake. I learned that she loved the water as much as I did, as she had grown up with water sports, like canoeing and water skiing, but had never learned to sail. Sailing and powerboating became a strong bond for us and our family throughout the years. It was several years later, through sailing, that I got to know Dave, the third man whom I mentioned in my testimony who helped lead me to the Lord.

A year and a half later, we were married; and right before our wedding, I was transferred from

Michigan to the Ohio territory. While the main office was located in a suburb of Cleveland, we decided in our first year of marriage to build a duplex in Bolivar, Ohio, so we could be closer to my parents and the lake. We moved to Bolivar a year later, and that was where we lived for twenty-four years. About three years after we were married and our oldest son, Bill, was six months old, Elise got a phone call that changed the direction of our lives forever. The small Baptist chapel in our community was participating in Campus Crusade for Christ's I Found It campaign. They were making random phone calls to people to talk to them about Christ and having a personal relationship with Him. Elise had been raised Catholic and was a devout churchgoer, but she had never learned about being born-again and what it meant to have a personal relationship with Jesus. She prayed the prayer of salvation that night on the phone. The next day the young gal who had called her stopped over to give her a New Living Translation of the Bible and to invite her to a women's Bible study in our community. When she told me what had happened, I was afraid that she was getting involved in a cult. I wasn't at all happy about her taking our son to the babysitter they provided at the Bible study. Looking back later, after I became a believer, I realized how that incident changed the eternal destination of most of our family—my sister-in-law Sandy, later my brother Jim and their two children, Jay and Julie, years later both of my parents, and of course our two sons, Bill and John. It was the women in Elise's Bible study that prayed for my salvation. Elise and I were unequally yoked for about eight years before I gave my life to Christ. This whole adventure could only have been orchestrated by God's guiding hand.

God also led my wife several years later to pray with my mother at the nursing home the day that she died. I was never really sure of where my mother was spiritually as I had only come to faith in Christ about two years before her passing, so we had never had that conversation about her salvation. As I mentioned previously, she had taught me to pray before bed when I was younger, and she would have liked to have attended church more regularly as a family. My mother was suffering from severe COPD and emphysema, having had asthma since she was a child. She had been hospitalized and then was transferred to a nursing home, where she had been for about two weeks. When Elise visited her, it was obvious that she was not doing well as she was extremely short of breath and had not been eating. Recognizing the seriousness of her condition, Elise asked her if she believed in Jesus and that He had died for her sins, to which she replied yes. Elise then prayed with her before she left. What a blessing! Upon hearing of my mother's condition, I arrived about two hours later with a milkshake, as I knew that she loved them. As I was giving her the milkshake, she asked me to hug her, which I found difficult to do because I never was much of a hugger. Fighting back tears, I told her that I loved her and that Jesus loved her. The staff then came in with her dinner and tried to encourage her to eat. She, unfortunately, began to aspirate; and before my dad could get there, she had passed away. My mother's death was a very significant turning point in my life, as after that day I did not fear death as much and I became much more of a hugger. It was definitely God's guiding hand that got me and my wife there that day!

As another example of God's guiding hand, I can now see how God was also preparing me, during those years in Ohio, for future ministry by giving me the opportunity to work with young people. I always had a love for young people, which led me to run for our local school board. Being on the school board for twelve years gave me the opportunity to chaperone many school events and to tutor several ninth-grade boys in math. During my sons' grade school years, I was able to coach their soccer team at the local YMCA. I felt compelled to pray with the team before each game, even though I was still a "baby" Christian myself. This was my first step in getting comfortable sharing my newfound faith even though it was with third, fourth, and fifth graders.

Two of the best years of my life were coaching my youngest son, John, in pee-wee football. I really enjoyed working with the fourth-, fifth-, and sixth-grade boys, and that time of bonding with my youngest son was really special, driving back and forth to practice and stopping for milkshakes on our way home. The Lord also helped to prepare me for future ministry through my hiring a number of young men from our local high school to work for me after school in my woodworking shop, making wood products for a division of Gowan Industries Inc. Our last summer in Ohio I taught the fifth- and sixth-grade boys at our church's Vacation Bible School, and the first several summers in Florida, my wife and I volunteered to teach the sixth-grade VBS class. All of this, plus the two years that we volunteered with the youth group, comprised of sixth to twelfth graders, were equipping me for becoming the youth director at our church here in Punta Gorda.

God also provided me during those years with a wonderful mentor named Jim, who was a retired pastor. I first met Jim because he "just happened" to buy one of the houses that we were interested in but could not submit an offer on as our house in Ohio still had not sold. Jim's house was only a few blocks from where we were building, and seeing that his boat lift was empty, I approached him about renting it for our boat until our lift could be installed. He informed me that he was in the process of buying a boat. But we soon got to be good friends as we both joined the local boat club and an investment club through our community civic association. Like the three men in my testimony, I grew to greatly admire Jim because of his deep love for the Lord, especially considering his family's hardships. If anyone could have become bitter toward God, Jim from the world's standpoint would have had just reason. He had three children, two sons and a daughter. Sadly both of his sons were born with cystic fibrosis, an incurable lung disease. One son died at the age of thirteen and the other at the age of nineteen. Jim and his wife later both developed cancer. He managed to survive non-Hodgkin's lymphoma and his wife, who praise God is still living at the time of this writing, is a two-time breast cancer survivor. Yet through all of these trials, Jim's faith remained strong. I was not the only one who greatly admired Jim, as he was named Hartford, Connecticut's Citizen of the Year in 1999 after he retired from pastoring a church there. I was privileged to get to listen to his powerful eulogy for his last son. He was a great encourager for me and frequently came over to pray with me in our home for the youth ministry. Looking back I can again see how God was guiding, preparing, and equipping me each step of the way.

While I was youth director, our associate pastor, who was my boss at the church, asked if my wife and I would be willing to start a young couple's small group. I felt totally inadequate to facilitate something like this, but he came alongside to help us get this group started. Because my wife and I have had a passion for helping young couples thrive in their marriages because of the struggles that we had experienced in our own marriage in those early years, we focused the small group's studies on finances, marriage, and parenting. God was guiding us to a future ministry, which we are still doing today, of mentoring couples prior to their getting married. Any couple getting married in our church is required to complete five sessions of mentoring. My wife and I had taken pre-Cana classes before we got married in the Catholic Church, which were good but not nearly in-depth enough. We wish we could have had the type of coaching then that is available to couples today, as it would have saved us a lot of struggles and disagreements. Marriage is hard work, and most couples are not prepared for the blending required of two individuals' temperaments and past lifestyles and the conflicts that will inevitably arise. Thanks to our pastor who asked us to start that young couples' small group, which then led to our doing pre-marital coaching, we have seen God's guiding hand leading us to a much better place in our own marriage.

CHAPTER 6

The Beat of a Different Drummer

Did you know that Jesus was considered a rebel in His time? While always honoring His Heavenly Father, He didn't always follow the customs, traditions, and culture of the day. Why? Because they were based on man-made rules and traditions that often were opposed to God's heart and His Word. The Pharisees and Sadducees made up laws to make themselves look better. Among other things, they were often hypocritical and more concerned with appearing to be good than obeying God. They were very legalistic, and so they often ignored God's message of mercy and grace.

In growing up I was pretty conservative and tried to follow the rules at home and at school. My dad was on the local school board for twelve years, starting my seventh-grade year, and I never wanted to embarrass or disappoint him. Having moved from Cleveland to New Philadelphia the summer before my fourth-grade year, it took me a while to make friends. Some cliques had already been formed, and I wasn't included in any of them. So I only had very few friends, which is very typical when a child has to change schools. I was never that coordinated and was small for my age, so when my mother insisted that I try out for Little League baseball in fourth grade, I did not even make the team. I tried again in fifth and sixth grade but didn't make the teams those years either. I was on the football team in the seventh and eighth grades, but there were seven strings with two guys left over, so you could say I was on the eighth string. Needless to say, I never got to play! My freshman year there were four strings and a few guys left over and I was one of them, and so I never got to play in a game that year either. I wasn't even going to try out for football my sophomore year, but a classmate, who was a starter, told me that he thought I was a better athlete than that and convinced me to give it one more try. The power of an encouraging word! With many backyard football games and lots of practice, I was able to work my way up to first string junior varsity and second string varsity. The poem "Don't Quit" that I quoted in chapter 2 certainly applies here. But I was never in the "in crowd" in junior high or high school, with the exception of maybe the fall of my senior year, since it was made up then, as it probably still is today, of your star athletes, cheerleaders, and those who were considered to be the "cool kids." The kids in the in-crowd often did really stupid things that in the long run they came to regret. I kept busy playing pool with friends, building model airplanes and boats, and pretty much just doing my own thing.

Again, because I never wanted to embarrass or disappoint my parents and because I knew that I had when I was forced to drop out of college my sophomore year, when I entered Kent State University, I was determined to succeed. By this time, I was twenty-two years old; and since I was still selling machine tools part-time, which required wearing a suit and tie, I frequently came to class dressed that way. Kent State University, at that time, was considered to be the second most radical school in the United States, and only the professors ever came dressed in a suit and tie. In my early business classes, there was a mix of students—your typical-age college students plus older students like myself, many of whom were Vietnam War veterans on the GI Bill. At first, when I came in a suit and tie, which was my more usual dress because of my job, I was definitely the odd man out. To my amazement, over time, more and more of my classmates started coming to class in sports coats and ties.

The lesson I learned was to not be afraid to be different and that I could be a positive influence on my peers. The Lord told Jeremiah in chapter 15, verse 19, "You are to influence them; do not let them influence you." God has us here to influence others in a positive way and, most importantly, for His kingdom. No matter how young you are, God can use you. As Paul wrote to Timothy, "Don't let anyone think little of you because you are young. Be their ideal; let them follow the way you teach and live; be a pattern for them in your love, your faith, and your clean thoughts" (1 Timothy 4:11).

Throughout your school years and later in your business and social life, there will always be others who will try to influence you for the world's values versus the Lord's. As followers of Christ, we have to decide whose voice we are going to listen to. As 1 Corinthians 10:21 says, "You cannot drink from the cup of the Lord and from the cup of demons, too. You cannot eat at the Lord's Table and at the table of demons, too." The footnote in my *Life Application Bible* explains it like this: "Are you leading two lives, trying to follow both Christ and the crowd? The Bible says you can't do both at the same time."

At this time, it is worth mentioning an old adage that goes, "You are who you hang with." So it is important to choose your friends wisely. Jesus

wants us to influence our unbelieving friends without them negatively influencing us, which can be
a challenge, especially in our younger years. We all
want to have friends, and we all want to feel like we
fit in. I felt some of that pressure my freshman year
in college, especially with it being my first experience away from home. But I still tried to continue to
do my own thing and not go along with the crowd.

After graduating from Kent State, I would come
home on the weekends and go sailing at a local lake.
That first summer I made friends with a local attorney and his wife and family, as they had their sailboat
docked next to mine. We became very close friends,
and on more than one occasion, his wife said to me
that she thought that I walked to "the beat of a different drummer." At the time, I really didn't think
a lot about what she meant by that; but in retrospect, I can see that she was right. I have always tried
to be my own person. Even though I didn't know
the Lord then, I have since come to realize that the
Lord wants us to follow Him and not conform to
the crowd. In other words, "walk to the beat of a
different drummer."

Matthew 5:14–16 teaches us that we are to be
salt and light to those around us. As salt, we are to
affect others positively, just as salt brings out the best
flavor in food. Like salt, if we become contaminated

by the world, we lose our saltiness. It is too easy for Christians to try to be just like everyone else and thereby lose their "saltiness." As I expressed in chapter 1, the three young men that helped lead me to the Lord had something different about them that I admired and respected. They weren't afraid to share their Christian faith in public and private ways, and I saw something in their lives that I wanted. Even though it took me until Dave came along to realize what it was. Regarding light, the footnote in my *Life Application Bible* for those verses says that "we hide our light by (1) being quiet when we should speak, (2) going along with the crowd, (3) denying the light, (4) letting sin dim our light, (5) not explaining our light to others, or (6) ignoring the needs of others." In all of these areas, I can give you examples of how I have failed at one time or another. But we are each a work in progress. And as a plaque in a friend's office said, "Be patient with me. God isn't finished with me yet." God has been more than patient with me through the years!

It is so easy for us, even as adults, to become influenced by the culture of the day, by what we see on TV, in the movies, on social media, by our friends, or by what we read. I have to continually ask myself, If Jesus were in the room, would He be pleased with what I am doing, watching, or reading? Colossians 2:8 says, "Don't let anyone lead you astray with empty philosophy and high-sounding nonsense that come from human thinking and from the evil powers of this world, and not from Christ." Taking the *road less traveled* can feel lonely at times, but in the long run, you will avoid a lot of pitfalls that can lead you away from God's best for your life. As I have grown older, I have found that spending time daily in God's Word has really helped me to better follow Christ and not follow my fellow man.

Most of us Christians are hesitant to share our faith with others or pray publicly before meals. But since my friend Dave powerfully influenced my decision for Christ by a simple prayer in a restaurant before his breakfast, I have tried to publicly offer thanks before meals, not only when I am with family but also when dining out with friends. I always ask their permission before I pray, and so far, no one has turned me down. I feel it is a simple way to acknowledge my gratitude to the Lord for all He has provided and to witness to them my Christian faith as I end the prayer, as we always should, with "In Jesus's name, I pray." I even had people come up to me at the restaurant, who were seated nearby, and say that they appreciated seeing a prayer publicly being said before a meal. This is just another way that we can be *different* for the Lord.

Romans 12:2 says, "Don't copy the behavior and customs of this world, but let God transform you into a new person by changing the way you think. Then you will know what God wants you to do and you will know how good and pleasing and perfect His will really is." Be a trendsetter! Be a rebel for Christ! Walk to the beat of a different drummer!

CHAPTER 7

The End Times and Our Legacy

Only God knows when the end times are coming, and none of us know when our own life will come to an end. The only certainty that we have is that each day that passes is one day closer to eternity. Knowing this, my desire is to continue to grow closer to the Lord each day. I want to have Jesus as my best friend! The scriptures tell us that Jesus will be our final judge as to where we will spend eternity and what our rewards will be for all eternity.

In chapter 1, I mentioned a young man named Roger, who was an Eagle Scout and who taught me how to swim. He went on to become a judge in our local court system. While I was serving on our local school board, our paths happened to cross again, which I would like to share with you. One of our high school teachers planned a trip for the senior class to New York City, as most of the students had never been out of the state of Ohio. Unfortunately, some of the seniors were caught with drugs in their rooms by one of the trip's chaperones. After calling their parents, they were sent back home on the next available flight. Our school policy at the time called for a semester's suspension. However, if the student received counseling, the suspension was reduced to something like a month. As the infraction occurred so close to the end of the school year, even though they had received the required counseling, graduation fell within that month's suspension period. This meant that the students would still graduate and receive their diploma, but they were not going to be able to participate in their graduation ceremony at the school. The parents were obviously extremely upset over the situation as they felt this was too severe a punishment. The superintendent and teachers involved expressed to the parents and students that if they had been caught by the NYC police, it would have been a felony on their record. I became involved as president of the school board when the parents of the students appealed to the school board. It was further distressing on my part as several of the parents had graduated from my high school just a few years ahead of me. Our superintendent supported the teacher, and the school's policy and the board agreed 5–0. The parents, at this point, tried to pressure several of the board members to change their minds; and two of them were about to concede. The superintendent and I were both in agreement that this would set a terrible precedent going forward, and the board held to our original decision. Not having been able to sway the board's decision, they felt their only recourse was to try to appeal the board's decision through the courts. As the board president, I was called to testify on behalf of the board in defense of our decision. Never having been in a courtroom situation before, I was some-what uneasy at the prospect of appearing on behalf of the school district. In a course of events that only God could have arranged, the presiding judge was none other than Roger, who had taught me how to swim at Scout camp, which gave me a sense of peace and comfort, knowing that he would be the one questioning me. Taking all of the testimonies into consideration, he ruled in favor of the school board. Knowing Roger, as an Eagle Scout and a man of integrity, I knew he would be an impartial judge. But his presence definitely helped me get through a very difficult situation.

The above illustration reminded me lately of how one day each of us will be called to stand before the ultimate judge, the Lord Jesus Christ. At that point, it will be very comforting to know that, as believers, we have a friend in Jesus who will judge us impartially. Once we are born-again believers, we have that peace and comfort of knowing that our sins have all been forgiven—past, present, and future. We will be declared *not guilty*, being covered by the blood of our Lord and Savior, Jesus Christ. We will, however, receive our eternal rewards based on the work that we have done in His name.

Second Timothy 3:1–5 says, "You should know this, Timothy, that in the last days there will be very difficult times. For people will love only themselves and their money. They will be boastful and proud, scoffing at God, disobedient to their parents, and ungrateful. They will consider nothing sacred. They will be unloving and unforgiving; they will slander others and have no self-control; they will be cruel and have no interest in what is good. They will betray their friends, be reckless, be puffed up with pride, and love pleasure rather than God. They will act as if they are religious, but they will reject the power that could make them godly. You must stay away from people like that."

Ever since Paul wrote those words to Timothy, each generation has wondered if they would be the one to see the Lord's return. While none of us know, we should all be living as if we are that generation and be prepared that, as Christians, we could experience persecution for our faith. As Jack Wilson, a missionary from our church to the Muslim world, explained to our youth group, our life on earth is like a pencil dot placed at the junction of where a wall meets the ceiling. Eternity is a line going around the room where the wall meets the ceiling over and over without ever stopping. Our life is so short in relation to eternity—a mere dot! We are all simply passing through. Another missionary explained to the teens that we are all really just backpackers journeying through life. This is not our real home! On a comforting note, there is an old saying that goes "We don't know what the future holds, but we know who holds the future."

Our legacy

Have you ever thought about your legacy? What kind of a legacy do you want to leave to your children and grandchildren? How do you want to be remembered? Have you ever thought that if you keep on doing what you are doing now, what impact will it have on your life five to ten years from now? What impact will it have on future generations—good or bad? These are important questions we should all be asking ourselves.

I was talking with my pastor a number of years ago, and he talked about the importance of leaving a godly legacy. This caused me to really ponder my legacy, and I have even asked a few family members and friends what they want their legacy to be. All of my friends have made a point of having a will or even a family trust, which is all fine and good. But making sure that our property, money, and any other assets are bequeathed to whom we wish should really be secondary to passing on the most important inheritance of all, our faith. God does not have any grandchildren. Each of us must come to faith in Jesus Christ on our own—in our own way and in God's timing. For some, it may happen as a child. For others, like my wife and myself, it may be as adults. I regret that building my true legacy did not begin until much later in my life. Our actions speak so much louder than our words. While I got into the habit of doing a daily devotional fairly early in my Christian walk, I failed to set an example for my sons of daily Bible reading. It wasn't until just recently that I set the goal of reading through the entire Bible and accomplishing that. It was actually my oldest son, Bill, who encouraged me to begin this by sending me an Old Testament reading from the book of Ezekiel that got me started when it should have been the other way around. I should have been the one encouraging my sons much earlier by my example. I praise God for how He worked through my son to help grow me.

When I look at life from this perspective, it changes how I spend my time and what I truly value. I have believed for a long time that we impact others on a daily basis in either a positive or negative way. In more recent years, I often pray that I am able to impact those with whom I come in contact positively for the Lord, which certainly includes my family members. I know that I have done this imperfectly but continue to ask the Lord to help me grow in this area of my life. I want to be that person that others see something different in, like the three friends who helped lead me to the Lord.

My wife and I have been praying for our sons and their families; first and foremost, that all of their names are written in the Lamb's Book of Life. We have been praying Colossians 1:9–10 back to the Lord for them, which says, "So ever since we first heard about you we have kept on praying and asking God to help you understand what he wants you to do; asking him to make you wise about spiritual things; and asking that the way you live will always please the Lord and honor him, so that you will always be doing good, kind things for others, while all the time you are learning to know God better and better." In Charles Stanley's *In Touch Devotional* for December 1, 2020, it asks, "Have you trusted Jesus as your personal Savior? Do you want to die confident and hopeful? The greatest legacy we can leave is not money or belongings but the truth that changes lives. Begin today to influence future generations by bringing them the good news." This is what has become my goal in life, and this is what I have attempted to do in writing this book.

CHAPTER 8

Things to Ponder

Solomon was considered the wisest man who ever lived. The Lord said to Solomon in 1 Kings 3:12, "I will give you what you asked for! I will give you a wise and understanding mind such as no one else has ever had or ever will have!" Solomon authored most of the book of Proverbs so that he could pass down some of his wisdom to future generations.

In Proverbs 1:7, Solomon wrote, "The fear [reverence] of the Lord is the beginning of wisdom." Throughout my life I have had a sincere reverence for the Lord, even before I became a believer. I have cringed when I have heard friends use the Lord's name disrespectfully. My fear of the Lord actually kept me from taking communion for years. While my theology at that time was incorrect, I didn't want to take communion improperly. I hate to admit it, but it wasn't until years after I became a Christian that I felt comfortable receiving communion. My wife, after many discussions, finally convinced me of the importance of receiving communion by sharing with me what Jesus said in John 6:53–54, "I assure you, unless you eat the flesh of the Son of Man and drink his blood, you cannot have eternal life within you. But those who eat my flesh and drink my blood have eternal life, and I will raise them at the last day." I finally took communion for the first time on Holy Thursday at a little Methodist church in Lakeside, Ohio. Receiving communion for the first time on Holy Thursday at a very moving service made it all that more special to me.

One of the promises from God's Word is that He will give us wisdom if we ask for it. In James 1:5 (NLT) it says, "If you need wisdom—if you want to know what God wants you to do, ask him, and he will gladly tell you; for he is always ready to give a bountiful supply of wisdom to all who ask him; he will not resent your asking." God's Word should always be our ultimate source of wisdom, as it says in 2 Timothy 4:6, "All Scripture is inspired by God and it's useful to teach us what is true and to make us realize what is wrong in our lives. It straightens us out and teaches us to do what is right." It is not what our pastors or Sunday school teachers or TV evangelists or what I say; our guide should always be

"What does the Bible say, what does the Bible say, what does the Bible say?"

To obtain godly wisdom, we need to be reading the Bible through the power of the indwelling presence of the Holy Spirit and with a seeking heart. We shouldn't be what is commonly called "pick and choose" Christians. This means we can't only choose to accept and follow the scriptures we like and reject or ignore those we don't like. We also need to guard against taking the scriptures out of context. Context means "the parts of something written or spoken that immediately precede and/or followed a word or passage and clarify its meaning." For example, in 1 Corinthians 15:32, Paul says, "If there is no resurrection, 'Let's feast and get drunk, for tomorrow we die.'" If you stop right there, you might think that Paul was implying that there is no resurrection and thus condoning a sinful lifestyle. But reading on in verse 34, Paul goes on to say, "Come to your senses and stop sinning. For to your shame I say that some of you don't even know God." Today we are seeing many trying to justify their sinful behavior by taking God's Word out of context.

We can, however, also glean some earthly wisdom from the writings and sayings of others. I would like to quote here several of the people I have found to be inspiring. One of those persons is Lou

Holtz, former head football coach of Notre Dame, who said in a commencement address at Franciscan University in Steubenville, Ohio, "There is never a right time to do the wrong thing. There is never a wrong time to do the right thing." James 4:17 says, "Remember too that knowing what is right to do and then not doing it is a sin." Another God-fearing man was my daughter-in-law Anne's grandfather whose favorite saying was "Keep the main thing, the main thing." In other words, keep God first and foremost in all that you do and say.

I would now like to share some quotations or sayings that have been especially meaningful to me over the years. Hopefully, they will impact your life positively the way that they have mine.

"How does my faith change the way I do things? How will I today preach the love of Jesus through my attitude and my actions?" We used this on a bookmark that we made for each of the teens in our youth group.

"The will of God will never take you where His grace cannot sustain you." Trusting that God is right there with us in every moment of our lives helps us to get through the tough times, like when our son John was diagnosed with cancer. Praise God that our son's cancer in his leg was encapsulated and he did

not require any chemotherapy or radiation after the surgery. When I began this book, John was also facing another health challenge that required an MRI. I praise God that nothing seriously wrong was found, and once again God calmed my fears. But we grieve for those parents and families whose outcomes were not positive ones. This is where our faith truly becomes tested, and we may never know this side of heaven an answer to our question of why. At times like this, trusting in God's goodness and resting in His arms of grace is all that we can do.

"Worry and faith cannot occupy the same space." Ever since I was a child, I have struggled with worry, especially when my dad would be gone on a business trip. In college, I worried a great deal about my grades. As I grew older, I worried about whether I would find a wife. This sin tendency continued to plague me, even as I grew in my Christian faith. As a young husband and father, I worried if I would be able to provide adequately for my family. Once our sons were out on their own, I continued to worry about their safety and well-being. But one of my bigger faith challenges came about five years after we moved to Florida when Punta Gorda was hit with a category 4 hurricane. Hurricane Charley caused an incredible amount of destruction to our little town with sustained winds of 145 miles per hour. We evac-

uated across the state for the hurricane, and I can remember telling my wife, as we drove home, that I feared our finances would be severely impacted by the damage from the storm. But God was faithful, and our insurance company paid for all the repairs to our home and boat. Hurricane Charley actually turned out to be a blessing in disguise for our city and for us personally, as our home and boat, after all of the repairs, were like new and our property's value actually rose. This was one of the bigger faith lessons in my life. Looking back and seeing how God has seen me through each worrisome situation, I have grown in my faith, knowing that He will see me through whatever the future might hold. I find that most elderly people have a tendency to worry even more than when they were younger. On the other hand, through prayer and reflection on God's faithfulness in the past, I have found myself worrying less. The phrase "Do not be afraid" is repeated more than any other phrase in the Bible. One scripture that especially has spoken to me is Philippians 4:6–7, which says, "Don't worry about anything, pray about everything. Tell God what you need and thank him for all he has done. If you do this, you will experience God's peace, which is far more wonderful than the human mind can understand. His peace will guard your hearts and minds as you live in Christ Jesus" (NLT). Worrying less, I have found a sense of peace and comfort that only could come from God.

"God does not call the qualified. He qualifies the called." A perfect example of this was our being called to lead our church youth group for five years with our having had no theological training. At my age at the time, I was also old enough to be most of the teens' grandfather. I questioned whether I had the knowledge or the stamina to do the job and I certainly was no public speaker, but God was faithful and blessed our ministry with significant growth over the five years. I prayed before every youth group and small group meeting that God would empower me to be able to speak into the lives of these young people. And my wife and I continue to pray for them today. Another example would be my feeling called to write this book. Who would ever have imagined that a young man who hated writing and struggled with English and had to take nine college English courses to complete the four required for his degree would be writing a book? Again, isn't God amazing? What an extraordinary God we serve!

"Our actions speak louder than our words." This one is not only valuable for us personally but can help us in evaluating the motives and true beliefs of others. There is another saying that goes along with

this same line of thinking: "If you're going to talk the talk, you better walk the walk." Do our words (or the words of others) align with how we are living our lives? We want others to be considerate of our feelings, but are we being considerate of theirs? Are we practicing what we preach, or are we being hypocrites? How we live can very easily contradict what we say.

"The Christian life is a life of balance." This is tough for most of us to achieve. I have struggled with this throughout my life. When I was in high school, football was my life. When my wife and I were first married, racing sailboats was my life. More recently being the director of our church youth group was my life. It is only recently that I have been able to achieve a more balanced life. This is probably due to the stage of life that I am now at, as I no longer have to juggle home life, work, church, and hobbies, like I did when I was younger.

"Don't be a holy huddle." It is easier, and often more comfortable, as Christians to only want to associate with fellow believers. We see this in many churches where people have few, if any, friends outside of their church. How can we influence unbelievers for the Lord if we never step outside of our comfort zone? Romans 10:13–14 says, "For anyone who calls on the name of the Lord will be saved. But

how can they call on him to save them unless they believe in him? And how can they believe in him if they have never heard about him? And how can they hear about him unless someone tells them?" Each one of us is called, as our pastor just recently said, to be "home missionaries," reaching out to our family, friends, neighbors, and colleagues. You don't have to travel outside of the country to be a missionary for Christ. Some suggestions for reaching others might be to ask if you can pray with them, in person or over the phone, when they are going through a tough time. Look for opportunities to talk about spiritual things and ask them questions about their beliefs. This may create an opening where you then can share your faith. I have had some successes at this and some failures as well. I missed a golden opportunity with a dear friend by not asking him more questions and instead giving him a lengthy discourse on Christianity that I realized later he wasn't ready to receive. While I prayed for him often, I was never given a second opportunity to share the gospel with him before his passing. A quotation from an unknown source, which we have posted in our kitchen, says, "If you want to be known the way Jesus was known as a friend of sinners, then you'll have to quit fishing from the boat and start swimming with the fish because fish rarely jump into the boat by themselves."

"Ask not what your country can do for you, but what you can do for your country." Former President John F. Kennedy said this in one of his more famous speeches. This is a great statement, especially today when many feel that they are entitled. In mentoring couples before marriage, I have taken this quotation and shown them how it can be applied to their marriage, stating instead, "Ask not what your spouse can do for you, but what you can do for your spouse." Most of us enter marriage from a very self-centered standpoint, thinking only about what our spouses can do for us instead of what we can do for our spouses. A Christ-centered marriage helps us to change our perspective and learn to put our spouse ahead of ourselves. Carrying this quotation one step further, I recently applied this to say, "Ask not what God can do for you, but what you can do for God." God gave us the greatest gift imaginable through the death of His Son on the cross as payment for our sins. Once we are saved, what can we do in return for God, not to earn our salvation but in gratitude for the gift of our salvation? Are we willing to answer His call on our life, wherever that might take us? Are we truly willing to serve Him?

"I will be happy when." This is a mental trap that I felt myself falling into at times, especially in my younger years. Not knowing Christ as my Lord and Savior, I did not have the contentment that He desires for us. It probably started off in high school with my thinking, "I'll be happy when I have a girl-friend." That was followed by "I'll be happy when I graduate from high school." While I did not look forward to my college years and I certainly struggled through them, I thought, "I'll be happy when I graduate from college." After college, I dated some, but the next big hurdle in my life was "I'll be happy when I find someone I can share my life with." Then there came "I'll be happy when we own our own home." While each of these brought short-term happiness, none of them brought long-lasting satisfaction. Very shortly after each, I would again start thinking, "I'll be happy when." With coming to Christ, I found a new sense of contentment that I had not experienced before. And I can honestly say that since then, I have had a major change of attitude and have become a very grateful and contented man. Like so many people, in my younger years, I didn't realize that I was playing the "I'll be happy when" game rather than being content and focusing on the many blessings that the Lord had given me.

This is one of the many lies that Satan uses to rob us of our joy!

"Do not be unequally yoked with an unbeliever." Second Corinthians 6:14–15 (NLT) says, "Don't be teamed with those who do not love the Lord, for what do the people of God have in common with the people of sin? How can light live with darkness? And what harmony can there be between Christ and the devil? How can a Christian be a partner with one who doesn't believe?" When we were first married, we were not unequally yoked, because neither of us was a born-again believer. But after Elise gave her life to Christ, about eight years before I did, there was turmoil and discord in our relationship during that time. The intimacy that Christ wants for marriage was not possible because we were not united spiritually. As the footnote for these verses in my Life Application Bible states, "Paul urged believers not to form binding relationships with non-believers because this might weaken their Christian commitment, integrity, or standards. Paul wanted believers to be active in their witness for Christ to nonbelievers, but they should not lock themselves into personal or business relationships which could cause them to compromise their faith." We praise God that both of our sons married born-again believers, and we sincerely pray that our grandchildren will

do likewise. It is truly a miracle and an answer to prayer that I eventually gave my life to Christ, as we know many couples who have remained unequally yoked. Most often it is the husband who refuses, for one reason or another, to commit, and the marriage suffers as a result.

"God is in control." Writing this book from 2020 to 2021 when it seems as if the world and our country were spinning out of control, it has helped me tremendously to know that, regardless of how things appear, our God has got this! None of this has taken Him by surprise! And He is using all of the circumstances of these years to accomplish His will and His goals. We simply need to rest in Him and know that He is in control.

Jackisms

The teens in our church youth group coined the following phrases as "Jackisms" because I said them so often.

"Sitting in a church doesn't make you a Christian, any more than sitting in a garage makes you a car." I first heard this expression from my landlord in Florida while we were building our house. Just because you

go to church doesn't mean that you have asked Jesus into your heart to be your Lord and Savior.

"Don't graduate from your faith when you graduate from high school." Too many of our young people lose their faith when they go off to college. Their professors and peers often ridicule their biblical worldview. Being away from the security of home and wanting to fit in, they allow the world to shape their thinking and their choices. While it is difficult in those years to stay strong in your faith, many young people are able to do so. As I shared in my testimony, the three men who influenced my life for Christ were all very strong in their faith through their college years and shaped the world around them, rather than let their peers shape them.

"Garbage in, garbage out." This is an old computer saying that means if you put incorrect information into a computer, you will get incorrect information out. Applying this to life means that what you fill your mind with is what is going to come out in your choices and your attitude. When we choose to fill our minds with God's Word, instead of the garbage being spewed through movies, books, the news, and social media, we will find that we make better life choices with fewer negative consequences. Another way of looking at "Garbage in, garbage out" was expressed by Nicky Gumbel in his *Bible in One*

Year 2021 for January 3. He says, "Evil starts in our thinking and imagination—that is, in our heart. It is a case of 'garbage in, garbage out.' We need to watch not just our actions but also our thoughts, attitudes, motives, and imagination. If you have been blessed by God, it is not for your own selfish indulgence or self-congratulation; it is in order that you can be a blessing to others."

"Are you willing to jump into the wheelbarrow?" I used this illustration with the teens to demonstrate what true faith really looks like, and I would ask them frequently after that if they were willing to get into the wheelbarrow. The story goes as follows:

> On July 15, 1859, Charles Blondin walked backward across a tightrope to Canada and returned pushing a wheelbarrow. The Blondin story is told that it was after pushing a wheelbarrow across while blindfolded that Blondin asked for some audience participation. The crowds had watched and "Ooooohed" and "Aaaaahed!" He had proven that he could do it; of that, there was no doubt. But now he was asking for a volunteer to get

into the wheelbarrow and take a ride across the falls with him! It is said that he asked his audience, "Do you believe I can carry a person across in this wheelbarrow?" Of course the crowd shouted that yes, they believed! It was then that Blondin posed the question—"Who will get in the wheelbarrow?" Of course... none did.

The story of Charles Blondin paints a real-life picture of what faith actually is. The crowd had watched his daring feats. They said they believed, but their actions proved they truly didn't. It's one thing for us to say we believe in God. It's true faith though when we *believe God* and put our faith and trust in His Son, Jesus Christ. (Creative Bible Study)

A closing thought

As I was completing this chapter, my daily devotional from Charles Stanley's *In Touch* devotional[4] led me to read Jude 1:17–25 with the heading "The Duty to Fight for God's Truth."

> Dear friends, remember what the apostles of our Lord Jesus Christ told you, that in the last times there would come these scoffers whose whole purpose in life is to enjoy themselves in every evil way imaginable. They stir up arguments; they love the evil things of the world; they do not have the Holy Spirit living in them. But you, dear friends, must build up your lives evermore strongly upon the foundation of our holy faith, learning to pray in the power and strength of the Holy Spirit. Stay always within the boundaries where God's love can reach and bless you. Wait patiently for the eternal life that our

---

4   Charles Stanley, *In Touch: Daily Readings for Devoted Living* (January 19–21, 2021).

Lord Jesus Christ and his mercy is going to give you. Try to help those who argue against you. Be merciful to those who doubt. Save some by snatching them as from the very flames of hell itself. And as for others, help them to find the Lord by being kind to them, but be careful that you yourselves aren't pulled along into their sins. Hate every trace of their sin while being merciful to them as sinners. And now—all glory to him who alone is God, who saves us through Jesus Christ our Lord; yes, splendor and majesty, all power and authority are his from the beginning; his they are and his they evermore shall be. And he is able to keep you from slipping and falling away, and to bring you, sinless and perfect, into his glorious presence with mighty shows of everlasting joy. Amen.

I was very moved by this scripture passage and thought how very appropriate for the difficult times we are living in today.

One last thing to ponder

With about 95 percent of this book completed, I told my wife that I was beginning to question whether I should finish this book and whether it was really worthy of publishing. I was also very much struggling for an ending as well. And I began to wonder if it would be of any benefit or value to my family and the reading audience. After all, as I said in chapter 1, I am just an ordinary man who has not accomplished anything out of the ordinary in my life. I am blessed with a great wife and two fantastic sons, two wonderful daughters-in-law, and four precious and special grandchildren, all of whom are gifts from God. God has given me far more than I deserve! God has also given me numerous opportunities to serve Him, some of which I accepted and some, I regret to say, I did not. So I asked the Lord to give me some kind of confirmation as to whether to continue this work to completion. I started praying in about the middle of December 2020, with COVID-19 still raging in Florida and throughout the country. And incredibly He answered my prayer for a sign on Christmas Eve! Our head pastor, four days before Christmas, unfortunately, tested positive for COVID-19, so he was unable to preach at all on Christmas Eve. He called one of our retired pastors,

Earl Smith, who had been my boss those years that I was youth director, to preach the 4:00 p.m. service being held outside in the park, which we attended. His sermon was entitled "Some Gifts of Christmas." Toward the end of his sermon, Pastor Earl said the following: "Bethlehem represents all that is ordinary and average in life. Most of us consider ourselves average, right? We're average height, average intellect, ordinary in our accomplishments, and of average skills. Guess what—God chooses to use the ordinary to accomplish *extra*ordinary things. Mary and Joseph were average and ordinary. The shepherds were average workmen of the day. The twelve disciples were just average guys. Christmas Eve was just another ordinary night. But God loves to take the average and make it shine. He takes the ordinary and makes it *extra*ordinary! That's His gift to you. So when you're feeling average, mediocre, mundane, and ordinary, that's when God can use you the most. Go figure! God doesn't use us for who we are but for who we can become when we walk through this life with Jesus. So here's what I suggest you do today. Receive the gift God is offering to you right now. It's the best Christmas gift ever! Accept the gift of the Christ child today and walk with Him into all of your tomorrows. That's the gift that you can give back to God!"

My wife and I turned to each other, and all we could do was smile and say, "What a confirmation to continue and what an answer to my prayer for an ending!" I could not have come up with anything better on my own! Pastor Earl's words were spot-on for all of us. God, You continue to amaze me! What an extraordinary God You are!

CHAPTER 9

Ending Thoughts and Thank-Yous

There is not enough time or space in this book, or any book for that matter, to give appropriate thanks to God for the *trillions of ways* that He has worked in my life. I want to start off first by saying thank you to God and how grateful I am for the following:

- Jesus dying for my salvation and God's for-giveness of all of my many sins
- God's coming into my life and giving me the gift of faith to receive His Son Jesus as my Lord and Savior;
- God's grace and mercy throughout the years toward me and my family
- My wonderful wife and our two wonderful sons and their salvation
- Our daughters-in-law for being born-again Christians, loving our sons, and raising our grandchildren in Christian homes

- Our four precious grandchildren, who I pray that all their names are written in the Lamb's Book of Life
- Being born in a home with two loving parents, who loved me and my siblings unconditionally
- My father-in-law and mother-in-law who passed the baton of faith on to my wife
- My parent's health, my health, and the health of my family
- Growing up in a small town and in a time when life was much simpler and safer
- Helping me to get a college education and a great job after graduation
- Providing me with godly role models, friends, and pastors to help me grow in my faith
- Leading us to a wonderful place to raise our sons, close to family, where they received a good education and a good start in life
- The business opportunities that were provided to me through the years
- Being born in a country with freedom of speech, freedom of religion, the right to bear arms, and such a high standard of living as compared to the rest of the world

- The opportunities this country has provided for me and our sons to earn a good living for our families

When I was ten or eleven, and all my thoughts were focused on football, I couldn't have imagined how God would bless my life with such a wonderful family and many incredible life experiences. I have truly been blessed beyond measure, and I am very grateful! God has truly been extraordinary in the life of this very ordinary man!

> Now glory by to God who by his mighty power at work within us is able to do far more than we could ever dare to ask or even dream of—infinitely beyond our highest prayers, desires, thoughts, or hopes. May he be given glory forever and ever through endless ages because of his master plan of salvation for the church through Jesus Christ. (Ephesians 3:20–21 NLT)

My final thought and prayer for my sons, their wives, my grandchildren, and those who read this book are the words of Jude 1:24–25, "And now all glory to him who alone is God, who saves us through Jesus Christ our Lord; yes, splendor and majesty, all power and authority are his from the beginning; his they are and his they evermore shall be. And he is able to keep you from slipping and falling away, and to bring you sinless and perfect into his glorious presence with almighty shouts of everlasting joy. Amen."

Acknowledgments

I would like to thank the following churches and their pastors for helping me to grow in my walk with Christ, for their insight and encouragement along the way, and for providing me the privilege of serving the Lord in a variety of capacities:

- The Bolivar Wesleyan Church and former Pastor Steve Gerig
- The First United Methodist Church of Punta Gorda and former Pastor John Bryant, former Pastor Earl Smith, and current Pastor Mike Loomis